CW00343606

This Other Salt

Aamer Hussein

This Other Salt

STORIES

Saqi Books

British Library Cataloguing-in-Publication Data
A catalogue record for this book is available from the
British Library

ISBN 0 86356 364 3 (pb)
ISBN 0 86356 379 1 (hb)

© Aamer Hussein, 1999

This edition first published 1999

Saqi Books
26 Westbourne Grove
London W2 5RH

Contents

This Other Salt

I'm running, through the long grass, down a slope that leads to the sea. The sun's about to set. A causeway of gold-edged steely light stretches across the darkening water, from sky to reddish sand. It's a holiday; I'm at the beach with my parents, ready to leave for the islands. Minutes before the boat departs, my mother tells my father to let me have some money for the apples I want to buy. She's dressed in green. My little sister, in her light blue sunsuit, clings to her hand. My father wears eggshell summer linen.

I'm ten.

I make my way to where the hawkers sit with piles of nuts, candy, plastic dolls. But I ignore their calls: I know what I'm looking for. The man with the parrot, who tells long stories and sells red apples.

— How much, I ask as I point to a big red apple.

— Two rupees. He holds up two fingers.

— You're joking. It's wormy. I'll give you eight annas.

He makes the V sign again.

— I'll pay you two rupees for your parrot.

— My parrot's a treasure. He tells stories about kings.

— He's made of cloth. He's got worms. He eats worms. You can feed him your apples: so there.

— But you can have this for free, he says, holding up a great green ripe pear.

And when I wake up, I'm thinking of Lamia: Lamia, who left Palestine when she was seven, and at thirty-four Beirut, where she had come of age and painted some of her most beautiful pictures. Exile after exile after exile: Egypt, Lebanon, Paris, London, New York and finally Indonesia. First with her Reuter-reporter husband; then, more often, alone in pursuit of new visions. After the civil war she wouldn't paint faces. She said their callousness made her retch. She painted in oils, seascapes and golden fruit; sculpted in stone, metal or clay and then painted her pieces in gold or other colours. She made me a golden pear for my thirtieth birthday, when I'd had the first of the recurring dreams. Golden Lamia, usually so optimistic, got very drunk with me one afternoon many years ago, soon after I'd told her I had to leave her, to look for what I'd lost in other places. She said:

— My paintings are shit. Lies and shit. There's no escape. I'll tell you the truth. That's all we have, you know.

— What, Lamia?

— Pain. It keeps us together. Not you, not me, I mean. Everyone. We're born in it and to it. Even when you think it's love, it's pain – it draws you together, makes you imagine you're two, separates you, tears you apart – you think it's love, but it's always pain, Sameer, only pain.

Then we began to make love on the carpet, but naked and joined to me she winced and flinched, pushed me out of her, pushed me away, and said:

— It hurts too much.

I took it for a physical reaction. I looked at her, naked with her small breasts and her wide hips, her thick wild hair knotted up because of the heat, and thought of how I'd told her once: When you're dressed, you look like an empress; when you're naked you're a goddess. I used to hang grapes in her hair. Afterwards we faked sleep in each other's arms. Now I'm not so sure what was hurting her, the coming together or the breaking apart, the fact or the metaphor. Probably both.

Nearly January: the last Saturday of another futile year. The winter hasn't chilled; it's what I call mushroom weather, like humid soup or mutton stew gone cold. It's been raining, in that distressed London way that keeps you locked indoors, watching junk TV, trying to read or work or think, smoking twenty cigarettes a day and downing half as many instant coffees, remembering other seasons, other spaces, too lazy or too tired to try leaving town. I decided not to go East this winter; told myself I couldn't afford it, that annual return as a privileged tourist playacting a homecoming, that vicarious living of other people's lives. I'd write instead. I suppose another reason for my hanging on is Tara. But I spend far too much time waiting for her, talking on the telephone, observing other people's pain, too lazy to live my own, too exhausted to search for it. I've finally found a temporary home: I live in a state of longing, all year round.

Come April I'll turn forty. My slim volume of stories has been out a year: a minor occurrence in my life, even an anticlimax. I dedicated it to Lamia, who died very quietly nearly two years ago, in the April that followed our farewell voyage. Cancer had already become her lover, that summer in Indonesia. We never met again, though she lived to see in her fifties. Her voice had faded and she'd started to limp, so they tell me, and she didn't want me to see her like that; with her reddish hair sparse again after chemotherapy, she wouldn't have. But the last time I spoke to her and told her love had come to nothing and I was still on my own and proud of it, she said she really wanted to see me give myself to one person, to stop being afraid that no one had enough to give because that only masked my own dread of giving myself up. Giving doesn't mean surrender, she said. Give someone a chance, and settle. Before I leave you forever, she meant. Michel, her journalist husband, with whom she'd argued so violently about politics and everything else, went back to her and nursed her in those last months. She died in Jakarta, a city she loathed. I think she wanted her body to be burned in Ubud, but in her final moments she decided that the serenity of Javanese faith gave her peace, and she lies in a Muslim cemetery she chose in Yogyakarta. Later, when he could travel to Palestine, Michel wished he had encouraged her to decide on cremation. He'd have taken some of her ashes to Beirut and their youth, and the rest back to Jerusalem to rest in the soil that gave birth to her. She went quietly, he told me over wine when I travelled to France to collect the paintings she left me. Quietly as she'd lived, I replied. I'm the only one who could tell them that they'd always imagined the sound of her footsteps, it didn't exist, she never made a sound.

And Hobnail, the erratic and inspired Anglo-Australian who spent the days of a summer season showing Lamia the distant secret places of South East Asia to subsidize his sex tourism and its nights hunting and buying young Asian flesh – Hobnail's dead too. How strange a pair they'd made, the frail grey-eyed auburn haired woman, dressed as a haute couture gipsy, graceful even in her fading, and the skinny bald man whose tight holiday denim didn't hide his growing pot, the two of them wandering around the sacred spots and ruins of Bali and Java.

In every city, Hobnail would find a lover, and that summer I was there with Lamia and he pursued us, we were burdened with his findings. Dinner here, dinner there, and he never had enough to pay. We were left to pick up the charges, for him and for his companion of the moment. From time to time, when he was bored, he'd try to force his stories on me or ask to share my room to save himself some money. His name was Hobbs. I called him Hobnail because he always intruded, heavy-booted, on my privacy. Lamia had called him Hannibal in a delicious Arab accent, with the emphasis and a guttural semi-vowel on the second syllable. Later, we had no other name for him but Hobnail.

But there's one scene that stays with me. We're on our way out of Jakarta. The companion of the moment arrives, Andy from Medan. Hobbs leaves us, spends some time with him until the announcer barks: Time to board for Denpasar. Michel runs towards them. There's a moment that looks like an altercation. Then money changes hands between Michel and Andy, the customary payoff. Hobbs joins them, comes back, and suddenly I understand him, though it'll take me months to believe that. It's his face I recognize: riven with pain, suddenly old, the ugly face of love.

His death did make a sound. OUR MAN IN SOUTH EAST ASIA BATTERED TO DEATH BY REFUGEE RENT BOY, shrieked the dailies. Scandals boiled in the tabloids. He'd come back to London to write a book about Indonesia. He was seeing Alex, an Eastern European man aged about twenty, someone he'd met outside a pub somewhere and taken up. Alex had asked for a light or a cigarette and Hobbs had realised that what he really wanted was a meal. He was starving, he smelt of poverty. Alex had assumed he was to reward the meal with little sexual favours. It wasn't really sex at all, Hobbs was to say, more a question of company and pity. But the pity dried up when Hobnail found out the guy was seriously on the game. Hanging around pubs and streetcorners, turning tricks for twenty quid a time, Alex had been picked up by someone in Oxford Street who turned out to be a plainclothesman and when he got shopped they found out, of course, that he was cheating on his dole and his application for refugee status was provisional. Alex passes on Hobnail's name as a contact. No good for a leading foreign correspondent still remembered for his youthful exposes of the Sukarno days. Hobnail refuses to acknowledge him. He doesn't want to know. So when Hobnail gets done on the way to his flat – battered to death, actually, with a dustbin lid, near Marchmont Street – it's the Bosnian who takes the blame. Actually Alex was a Rumanian, but he lived the way people here expect Bosnians to live, or Algerians, so the tabloids left out the Bucharest bit.

Somehow, I don't believe Alex killed Hobbs, though his defence of himself wasn't very convincing. He looked too hapless – in contrast to Hobnail's sharp-toothed Balinese boys – that time Hobbs had turned up with him at a booksigning I did. I'd had to talk to them, though I didn't want to. I remember the boy had bad teeth, two or three of them were blackened or gold, and I wondered why Hobbs hadn't forced him to have a bath before bringing him out in public. Alex: I remembered his name for the way Hobbs had said it, in that manner he had, which announced someone permanently, helplessly enthralled by love. Perhaps Hobbs had reprimanded Alex, played the putative father, said the unsayable. Perhaps there'd been an accident.

I wonder whom Hobbs loved when he died: or if it was his hunger, that endless hunger I'd seen in his eyes the morning at the airport, that led him to take home with him someone who was strong enough to brandish iron. Because that's how it went, the reported story. People had seen him walk down from Russell Square to his apartment block with a small young man. They hadn't seen his companion's features, because he had on a jacket with a hood, like Alex's jacket of cheap pink imitation silk.

ა⁀⚙︎⁀ა

Colours looked different to Lamia in the last months of her life: she was always in search of reds, and fire entranced her. Indonesia had made her paint faces and figures again. She did a series of nude bathers on the banks of the Ayung river: she always thought the miniatures were incomplete. I wonder what Michel has done with them. He couldn't understand her work, couldn't keep up with the changes of her vision.

I suppose it was in search of fire that Hobnail took us to a royal cremation in Gyanyar. The funeral pyre was high. Ceremonies lasted till nightfall, with fires blazing all around us. Families had exhumed their hastily buried dead, to consign them to the flames on this omened day. The hawkers were out in hordes, peddling nuts, handicrafts, fried food rolled up in banana leaves. Beers changed price as you bargained. A little boy adopted me: he played with my shoes, and sat quietly in front of me for a long time. He got up only once, to urinate. He refused food. Finally, he accepted a rambutan from my shoulder bag, and turned his back to me to eat it. Lamia sketched in a trance. I was trying to avoid the scent of death: in pagan Bali, it mingles with the perfume of cempaka and cloves. I could see death in

Lamia's eyes. I didn't want to know. I wrote a postcard to Tara, wanting her to see Bali as I saw it. I bought the Ramayana sketched on a palm-leaf scroll for her that day, from a woman who tried to speak to me in Sanskrit. By sunset Lamia was exhausted. We couldn't see Hobnail anywhere. Lamia suddenly became restless. Hot, she wanted a long shower. Then I found Hobbs under a wall, rapturous in attempted intimacies with a giggling Wisnu Darmawan. Wisnu was the tall young assistant manager at our Ubud hotel; requisitioned by Hobbs to be our guide in Bali, he was as lost in Gyanyar as we were.

Though he had the name of the Hindu god who came to earth as the Balinese hero Rama, Wisnu was a Javanese migrant and, he'd affirm, the son of pious Muslims. He'd been on the island about a year. His only contribution to our excursion was to take turns with Hobbs at the wheel of the Kijang, and every time we stopped for a drink or a walk he'd look for creepers bearing flowers that shrank when they were touched. He called them shy princesses. Once Hobbs made the unforgiveable mistake of asking where the best roast pig in Bali was to be found. Wisnu paled.

— Too many porks in Bali everywhere, he muttered. Balinese people keeping too many porks. We don't keep porks in Jogja. Only Chinese people growing porks in Java.

We realized he liked Lamia and me because he thought of us as people of the Koran. Lamia told me she found him so exquisite she wanted to paint him as a half-naked Solonese court dancer. She had her way: he appeared in a sarong one evening at the Ayung. He'd probably put away his scruples about the shameless infidel Balinese because of the heat. She did a beautiful gouache impression of him in movement, gold and ochre and white: the hands and eyes and the tilt of the head were all his. Later, when I saw the Ramayana performed in the kraton of Yogyakarta, I could see: the dancer who played Rama, in his height and limbs and smile, could have been Wisnu Darmawan's twin. Maybe Lamia had seen Wisnu through Hobnail's eyes: it was Hobbs who looked up at Wisnu as though he were a god.

While Lamia slept, I'd sit on the terrace, smoke my clove-rich kreteks and draft my story – or think about it. It was inspired by something that had happened to me in Leyden, the year before. I had left Suhayla, my on-again, off-again lover of the time, in London. Lamia and I were spending a few days in a flat that had been lent to us by a friend. Below our windows, the swan-speckled river sluggishly ran. It was Easter. We'd been told that someone had committed suicide there, not long before. The first night we were there, we couldn't sleep. The wind blew savage outside and the rain screamed. Lights switched themselves on and off and the bathroom was so cold it was impossible to go in. Lamia, usually intrepid, was trying to remember the prayers of protection she'd long since rejected. The next night was rainier and the atmosphere even more tumultuous. A terrible banging came from the direction of the front door. But there was nothing I could see. I finally went into the bathroom. A window hung loose on its hinge, as if a night-thief had just escaped. A cloud of clove-scented smoke hung in the air. In the morning, our host – a Dutchwomam married to a Sumatran poet – came back from Rotterdam. She told us that the flat's former tenant had been an Indo called Mellema, who'd slashed his wrists in the bath. They'd called in an exorcist, but the restless spirit remained restless. We moved to a hotel that evening.

Being in Ubud brought back the story to me. Every night, I'd find on my bed there a straw puppet of Sri Dewi, the local rice-goddess, its head on my pillow. Somehow the faint repulsion the idol evoked in me brought back the Leyden incident, and those horrible huge dolls young men in Italian towns buy for their girlfriends at Christmas. I thought how effective it would be to write a story with other stories concealed in it, a ghost story, post-modern Stephen King. A couple on the verge of parting arrive at a Balinese chalet where an Indo with the personality of Hobnail had killed himself the year before, driven mad with love for a native called Putu or Ketut or Wayan who would have the features of Wisnu Darmawan.

Hobbs, too, had an eerie story about Bali. His own wife, a promising anthropologist, had died there, by her own hand or so it seemed, in the late sixties. Too much death and sorcery here, Hobbs would ominously say, hinting at devilry and murder. I couldn't help thinking that Elisa Kendall-Hobbs must have caught her young husband with a Balinese lover. I'd bring all that in, a flashback. The tale within the tale would be narrated by the Balinese. The wife – I'd give her Tara's face.

The vagaries of Garuda's bookings meant that Lamia left for Yogya one night before I did. I sat on the terrace by the pool, drinking iced arak and brem. When Hobnail came to join me, beer in hand, I was honest: I'm trying to write. Late that night as I sat on the terrace with a bottle of Perrier and my kretek, trying to transform Hobnail into a suicidal Indo besotted with a native he thinks is possessed by his dead wife, someone knocked on the chalet door. I wrapped my robe around my half-bare body, impatient: I thought the importunate Hobnail was lonely, and drunk enough to risk rebuffal. I don't think he'd got very far with Wisnu, who probably accepted his few cheap favours with a smile and customary Javanese grace. Invaded by my characters, I thought, and I wasn't wrong. I opened the door to a laughing, bowing Wisnu, a Balinese jacket and sarong incongruous on his tall frame. He had a frangipani behind one ear.

— I didn't ask for anything.

— Champagne. He smiled.

— I think you have the wrong chalet, I said. Mr. Hobbs is two doors down.

— Compliments of the management, he said, and pushed past me with champagne and seasonal fruits on a tray he set down on the table: mangoes and mangosteens, miniature bananas, rambutan, grapes, pears and a pineapple.

It was my last night on the island. He was already opening the bottle. I felt I should offer him some of the champagne. I knew he wasn't a waiter and he'd been willing to help us all through our stay. He accepted the glass silently. He talked all night. He had a wife and a son in Yogya. He was going back, taking the plane tomorrow, to be there during the Mouloud festivities for the Prophet's birthday. He should have left for town hours ago: that's where he had been living. I told him he could go down to Denpasar with me if he liked, in Hobnail's jeep, hired at Lamia's expense. He should wait at the gate. We rested a little: I on the bed where Lamia had lain only hours before, he on mine. He left as dawn broke, barefoot through the French window over the damp grass between the overhanging banana leaves. I sluiced myself with water from a barrel in the outdoor sunken bath, naked under the open sky, leaves squelching beneath my feet. I watched a tiny olive lizard I'd dislodged run up a betel-palm.

On the way to the airport, Hobnail's eyes and smiles had little chains of knives in them.

— What was he like? he asked me at the airport. Wisnu had discreetly removed himself, to buy cans of cold beer, I think.

— Who?

— Don't act the innocent, Sameer. Was he good? I saw Wisnu leave your room this morning.

— Did you really now? Not bad, I sneered. Not bad at all. (Let him keep his fantasies, I thought. If Wisnu had wanted to give more than I was willing to take, I hadn't been prepared to notice. Sometimes, since, I've wondered what all the fruits were for. He would say with disdain of Hobbs: Not good, paying for poor boys like that. Spoiling them. Making trouble.)

In Yogyakarta, Wisnu got in touch and drove Lamia and me out to Solo and Candi Sukuh, and showed us some of the most beautiful little mosques in town. Lamia loved them, because men and women prayed there side by side. The act of prayer was a simple part of living. He drove us through villages that were really slums pock-marked with poverty. He took me to the finest foodstalls. I remember the nasi gudeg we ate with our fingers the night I left, rice lush with spices and jackfruit. He still writes. But for a while I haven't replied.

∾ ⚙ ∾

I never wrote the Balinese ghost story I'd planned. Hobbs couldn't make the transition into a haunted Eurasian; death and realities got in the way. Handsome Wisnu and Ubud aren't in my book. I finished it instead with fictions carved out of my own life. I wrote about the fallen smell of fruit: gold papaya flesh spilling over marbled green skin on to white stone, ants ravishing its fallen sweetness. About the fallen smell of rain, the vapour rising off my skin as I stood in the melon patch burning with the freshness of the shower. About the fallen music of the past, its shattered notes calling out the night's name, the name of someone I had lost which once was Layla, like a woman singing or the sea breaking into white foam on white rocks, like the rain on a May night. I wrote about the city by the sea, hers and mine. Of home as a forgotten song, a shared language, common consummation like bread. I wrote about my longing for another tongue, a mother tongue, the language of my longings: liquid, whispering, sibilant. I suppose by the time I reached its end I knew the call of home was gone, I had written about a Karachi that was lost, that I had left twenty-five years ago, and then I was looking for light again. But my book ended with images of all my cities on fire. Karachi had been in flames for years. I knew I couldn't keep on grieving for that contagion. Then Bombay, too, that other city by the sea that had served for years as a surrogate home, was in mourning the last time I was there a year ago, for the riots that had ravaged it a year to the day before. I'd thought of going on to Pakistan, but at the airport I changed my ticket and stopped for a night at an unfamiliar city in the Gulf. There I could see the sea and the sand of remembered places.

When I came back my mirrors of belonging had cracked, because I hadn't been able to see my face in them. In London, too, the cracks in the painted glass were widening. Lamia had been dead almost a year. I tried to reach out to Tara, even to lean on her, though I'd been trying to renounce all hope of winning her. But she couldn't carry my widening despair for more than a day. Tara, though she wasn't even born there, kept returning to Karachi every year and brought back reports of a city that wasn't mine, that I have to let go of.

Tara was putting down deeper roots in London, locating herself in a rhetorical space of blackness that had little resonance for me. She fell in love with an ugly, wild-haired, bisexually charismatic performance poet – more of a stand-up comic, really, who celebrated ethnic music and cooking. Kim also told jokes about SM and dykes and leather that I couldn't pretend to understand. She wrote politically incorrect ditties about hybrids, which because she was mixed race herself made me laugh unwillingly when Tara dragged me – or I dragged myself behind her – to a joint in the East End to see her perform.

So now I'm trying to work on something else, something that holds off thoughts of Hobbs and his life and death; something kinder, a story that keeps me in the light, or perhaps the light on me: a critical biography of an intriguing couple from Lahore, writers at the turn of the century, who ran their own press and published their own novels and stories. An idealized life, almost a myth, into which I could imagine myself and Tara. With a suitably tragic end that I could have done without, though: the wife died at the age of thirty. Tara turned twenty-seven last June. She's changed from the Tara of two years ago, with her scholastic inclinations and her preoccupation with political movements and social causes. Tara once planned to go home and crusade for women's rights, minority rights, the rights of the poor. She tried out Islamabad: she lasted a month. But right now it's love and money she cares about. She works for a leading production company, uses her academic credentials. Tara will live forever. It's Lamia who died young. Michel told me that Wisnu was one of her pallbearers. His family keep an eye on her grave.

There's another part to my dream: post-intermission. When I look at the shore, I see my parents, wildly waving:

— Come on now, you'll miss the boat, they seem to say.

As I run down the slope to the sea, I trip on a rock, lose a slipper.

If I run on (I think) my mother will scold me for losing my sandal; if I stop to look for it, I'll miss the boat. Trouble either way. Finding it, at least, will show her I'm responsible, a man. But that can come later. The sky's nearly dark, but I'm not afraid of the falling night. I want my pear. I dig my teeth into its tart freshness. I look at the boats, which wave their bright banners, on their way to distant islands. When I finish my fruit, I'll dig my fingers and toes into the taut, moist sand, I'll build a fortress, I'll write my name or a story.

I've never really understood this part of the dream: and there's no long grass on Karachi's beaches. Maybe my dreamscape is the shore of Beirut, or a riverbank in Bali. All I hear when I wake is the sound of the sea of tongues: *père* leaves son, leaves with *mère* by *mer*; son devours pear (fruit or father) with one foot bare. One shoe of identity gone from my foot (in my mother tongue, *pair*). So in the end, it's a dream about parents and words, and about being alone, and I'm sure Lamia's there, too, because she spoke perfect French and painted fruit and spent her life between land and sea. Because remembered love always tastes like the fruit of Eden, flavoured with the forbidden, threatening as incest. Dark feelings fall, even on my search for light. No Manichaeism for me, as I say to my friend Maryam who tells me of the sequence of poems about light she's writing. Sometimes it's easier to deal with death than with desertion, so my visions find their way into the true story I'm researching: icons of Lamia, lurid red posters of Tara, images of myself, finally loved, finally loving.

It's the last day of the year. One of those days when things keep inventing themselves around you, so that you're always one step behind the day. You feel needed, maybe even wanted. That's usually because you've planned with such care, of course, not to stay alone. So the things you really wanted to do, the places you wanted to be in, don't remember you. And if they do, it's too late. I've revolved like a 45 rpm all day. I'm hyperventilating.

This time, though, I thought it wasn't going to be that way. Kim's been cheating on Tara for days, can't settle down, plays around, wants

to fly, wants to be chained. Last week Tara chased Kim out. Told her
to clean up her act, get her head examined. And then she spent days in
agony, cramped with menstrual or pre-menstrual tensions, crippled
with doubt and need. My moment to step in. Only, I said to myself,
because I'm lonely, and so is she; I gave up on anything other than
friendships and celibacy two years ago. If I have a companion now, it's
Lamia – the Lamia of thirteen years ago, merged with the Lamia of
Bali. I see her pale small foot, white and gold at the same time,
remember looking at it and touching it, feeling then that I'd once
known a love, for her, so unbearable that I'd had to destroy it before
it destroyed me, I'd had to go away and tell her I was going, and there
in our Ubud chalet I knew that it was still unbearable, that if anything
my desire for Tara made me love Lamia more, without need or
anxiety. I knew, too, that the fresh desire was born of that earlier
passion, younger and more raw, it was a replay and a re-enactment, I
knew that if I hadn't been broken and ridden and broken again by
Lamia all the way from Istanbul to Christmas I'd never have imagined
loving Tara at all. I kissed Lamia's foot there and cried hoping that my
tears wouldn't awaken her and yet wanting her to know that I wasn't
crying for her death, which I knew would come soon, but because all
my love for her was in this other salt, more than it had ever been in all
the anguished saline love I'd poured into her nights, and I had to give
it to her before she went, it was too heavy for me to carry, all this
bitter, crystal salt, without her in the world. I think she knew, because
after a tactful silence she opened her eyes and asked for a pillow and
a glass of water and when I brought them to her she said:

— Couldn't you just die here, with all this around you? I want to
be burnt here. Or buried in the mountains.

I looked through the open sliding screen doors and saw tall trees,
flowers white yellow and red ensconced like candle-flames high high
above us in the green, turquoise sky and fiery rocks bending over
them, the roaring silver Ayung river below. The air was full of life:
dragonflies, spiders spinning from branch to branch, black little birds.
And I knew I still wanted to live, even without her, even if living set me
on fire.

In Ubud the scent of clove was overpowering. Bougainvillaea bloomed in such profusion we forgot to count its colours. (Now and then we see a wild and earnest rose. Rice terraces fall from the sky, green proud stalks rising from ponds that white ducks swim on. Water nestles in the navels of proud hills chiselled from the belly of God.) At night I sat among the mosquitoes, daring them to take me, challenging their venom with mine. Fireflies rose towards the waning moon. Soon after sunset the musicians would set up their threnodies. The flute mourned over the clinking aphonic keys of the gamelan. (Earlier, in the afternoon, the same melody plays for the butterfly troupe of little girls from the ballet school. Shoulders out, hands twisting, the children dance, to the clapping and the lero-lero-lero chanted by their maestro.) The fragrance of frangipani filled the air; each musician had a flower tucked behind an ear. (Between rehearsals, the children run to the ornamental pond to scoop up tadpoles and little fish in their palms. Once on the mountain path a child approaches us and points, wordless, to our basket. Lamia thinks he wants her mineral water. Angur, angur, he finally says: the word for grapes is the same in his tongue and mine.) And there on the mountain as the colours of the day flowed into each other I'd think about love. Or the lack of it, the gap where need might be. I still wonder what the words of the song meant – the lero-lero-lero of the afternoon's chant transposed into words in the evening, possibly words of love. (I'm walking down the hill to the Ayung when I first hear the song. It's afternoon. The hill is steep and I'm drenched in sweat, slipping in my soft leather shoes. Lamia, that fish, has changed her form. She leaps down the pathway like a goat, perhaps to prove that illness hasn't vanquished her. At the river the naked old women soak their sagging breasts in the sun while sons brush their teeth and daughters-in-law in fancy underthings wash clothes. A young woman pulls me into the river, helping me down the stones with the strength of two men. Soon I'm in the water with the bathers. Lamia sits on a rock, talking to a sarong-soaked Wisnu. Drops and rivulets glisten on bare backs brown and black. The fierce light burns my arms an even deeper bronze. I clear the water to join Lamia. For a moment I think she's sleeping. When I'm wreathed in the clove-heavy smoke of my silent cigarette she starts talking. Then I tell her about Tara, how I met her one night at a club I'd been dragged to by friends and how since then that she's never gone away. But Lamia's looking at Wisnu, who's taken my place in the water. For an instant, something shoots through me: perhaps I miss someone).

I thought of the preparations we were making for her dying, of Lamia leaving me forever and of the pain I'd never really learnt to feel, the pain of someone leaving, maybe that's what you call love. But for me, with Lamia no longer mine, absent but close, it was there and it was something else, I wouldn't call out to it or give it a name. It was something that stayed, it melted into the colours and the birdsong and the light rain, it cried in the night and pulled me close to shadows I wouldn't see in daylight. It called when the day was ending, when the sky changed from blood-orange to purple smoke, beckoned to me when the first two stars emerged, became a third star. It couldn't obscure the moon, it was the moon.

I'd never understood the kind of love that needs one person. I felt desire grew in me, I carried it within myself. Maybe that was Lamia's gift, that desire for the sky, the colours and the changing and the light, for the pain and everything that went with it. When you're in a place so strange to you, far from everything you know, when you travel at all, you lose your skins one by one until only the seventh and innermost layer is left, you become nothing. You see your future as some kind of dream you can stage yourself. That's one of the gifts of being nothing any more. So I went back to London longing for Tara or for my dreams of her and of what I could be for her, prepared to give her what I had, only to find that she'd already come as close to me as she ever would. But some part of her was still there, tied to me, her loneliness, maybe, and the recognition of mine, or some vestige of desire. You often respond to those who want you, so strongly that your desire overtakes the original plea for attention. Tara must feel something, atavistic or primitive, for a man who wanted her, without visible demands or naked desire.

∾✥∾

... 'A Quiet House.' A poem by Charlotte Mew, copied out in Tara's hand in one of my notebooks. She recited it to me two months after we met, the first time I told her about splitting with Suhayla the year before, about how destructive a relationship can be even when you're not in love; how it leaves you pitted and scarred, even for a little while. Shell-shocked, I said I was.

> Red is the strangest pain to bear,
> In Spring the leaves on the budding trees;
> In Summer the roses are worse than these;
> More terrible than they are sweet:
> A rose can stab you across the street
> Deeper than any knife ...

— But red doesn't hurt me at all, I told Tara when I came back from Indonesia. It makes me think of Bali and living.

Me with my memories of Lamia, Tara with the quarrelling spectre of Kim – two solitudes, spending the last nights of December eating nuts and crisps in dismal yellow North London pubs, watching dingy comedies in local cinemas and coming out empathy-fatigued, with little left to talk about, waiting for a suitable moment to say goodbye. I've been playing the consoler or confessor, or trying to; loving vicariously, wondering whether this is better than the emptiness I've become so used to living. Anyway, it can't be much worse. At least I'm trying to give, make myself useful, tell myself I should be unselfish. And emptiness has something in common with vicarious sexless love: there's something burning, a torch or a bush, on the other side of the white chasm in front of the confessor and the confider, something that calls you, tells you that you, too, will come to it in time.

I never speak to Tara about Lamia. We've planned to bring the New Year in together, quietly, at the Mata Hari – Eye of the Morning

– a kitsch miniature evocation of an Orientalist's South East Asia. We'll eat the weirdest *fruits de mer*, or flambéed prawns, smoke kreteks and drink champagne. Maybe we'll even learn something new about love.

Tara's been red-hot with love all summer, all autumn – now, as the year dies, she's blue. There's that sultry saxophone whine in her voice again, phrasing endless minimalist improvisations on two notes: Love and pain, pain and love. Sometimes I think she feels she's the only one conversant with them, she's the expert but also the expert sufferer. The martyr who knows the price of joy, who knows that lovemaking is always painful, always relinquishing, an act of renunciation even when it's meant to be taking, a little bite of death. Sometimes I agree with her, add my fewer, broader notes to hers. Usually I'm in counterpoint, sweeter or more salt, always patient. Sometimes I think I'll suffocate with patience. Dying's actually no problem. It's the way there that's so fucking long, so full of mirages that make me want to live again. Closer to mercy or oblivion, every winter, step by rheumatic step, I listen, I wait, I watch, I write, always talking, forever silent.

Tara's blues may be gone, though, at least for a while. Kim's back. She swears she'll stay forever, however short that is, this time. But our night on the town's still on: *à trois*. So Tara tells me now. She asks, on the phone, just a couple of hours before we're meant to meet:

— Can Kim come with us? Otherwise she'll have to hang out with tramps in some club. She'll drive us.

Tara's voice on the wire carries in it the clash of quiet cymbals, the triumphant click of castanets. Perhaps, I think cynically, it's because I'm said to have some money in the bank. More likely it's Tara's sense of fair play. And anticipation of the other game, less fair and more enthralling; the adventure of being with two people who love her, who will court each other to gain her favour, protect her from each other. Mistress of the night, triumphant harbinger of the coming year, she'll reign supreme.

∾ ⊛ ∾

I can't help feeling there's something predatory about Kim, something ready for the occasion, any occasion. Even on a night like this, when she's working to please. Or maybe a night like this is what reveals the mercenary in her. Her eyes scan the prices on the menu. She orders a whole fish and the most expensive wine. Tara shrinks and smiles and I wave my hand in courteous dismissal. Our table, in a black glass cage, is small and fragile. Tawdry souvenirs of Java and Bali surround us, rice fields and bare-breasted Balinese on fake tapestries in faint green and coral shades, painted bright lamps, hideous leather puppets. Masks slip and are replaced.

— Let's go there together; we must, we have to, Kim says when Tara begins to recount my stories of Bali and Java. We dance into plans and projects: Borobudur, Prambanan, Yogyakarta, and somewhere in Sumatra, maybe Tapanuli or Lake Toba.

— Desire – Tara is conflating trajectory and text – Desire, Sameer, you write about desire in those stories of yours, they're your best, when you talk about love in a man's voice it could still be me, and all the women in your stories are me and still they're you. I would say it's always desire you write about.

— And what about depression? I think I write out of depression. Other peoples'. And about how they depress me too. And don't I write about death? (Hobnail's boots ride my brain again. Funeral pyres burn high in Gyanyar. In a cemetery in Yogya, Lamia's name in Arabic and Latin letters.) And love? In my next story I'm going to write about love again. It's an epic romance called 'Silken Nights'. Once upon a time there was a Mughal emperor who went to a New Year's feast where he fell in love with a beautiful widow who sold him a ring. For days he pined for her until the Queen his wife who loved him so much she would for him have sacrificed her life told him to take the beauteous lady to his marriage bed. But I cannot betray the lady mother of my fine sons and my pious daughters for a mere whim of lust, said the emperor. No, quoth the Queen his wife, it is, in our faith, a kind duty to protect the weak. To give the widow shelter befits your virtue and glory. So the Emperor married the fair widow. But some months later the Queen, so it is whispered in the corridors of Agra's fort, poisoned her rival with a garland of red, red roses. And the Emperor lived happily ever after with the Queen, notwithstanding occasional fornications, until she died and then he built the splendid Taj Mahal to shelter her mortal remains. And he wept all the remaining days of his life, with little maidens beside him to wipe his tears with their perfumed hair. The story is narrated by an immortal green parrot . . .

— Shut up, stop it, you lying swine, you'd never stoop so low . . . (Tara's choking on her drink.)

— I didn't know Sameer could be so ironical, I've never heard Sameer being so ironical. (Kim has emerged, dazed, from her unaccustomed silence.)

— *Cin cin*, I shout. Let's drink to four letter words like l-o-v-e. To pop-song cant. To that pain in the arse.

Tara's laughter, or too much smoke and sparkling grape, is making her cry. Or tears are running down her face because she thinks I'm aching for Lamia. Maybe because the colour red is all she ever sees. Then I write on a paper napkin which I slide over the table to Kim:

— If you ever hurt Tara, I will kill you.

But what I suppose I mean is, I'll kill you if you ever take all of her away from me. We're hamming it up for all we're worth, the trusty trio. I can't deny there's something dangerous about this, dangerous because our embracing and caressing and touching and kissing, in the midst of strangers saluting each other and shouting while they bury December, has something erotic about it, an eroticism that's masochistic, hardly sexual at all, like public nakedness, like an unwillingly witnessed copulation. Tara's in my arms, her back against my breast, my breath grazing her left cheek, my left arm around her ribs, stroking her right side. Kim holds my right hand. I kiss the corner of Tara's mouth. Her dangling silver earring tickles my cheek. Soon her hair will make me sneeze. But she turns her head.

— Happy New Year.

I'm being kissed on the mouth by pairs of lips that have loved and kissed each other. Touched by hands that pass on leftover love.

Hobnail hides in us all, I think with the irrelevant wisdom of near-drunkenness. He dies in our eyes. It's one of those rare tipsy insights that actually make sense. It's not the buying and the selling that counts. It's the desperation of holding on to someone for fear of being abandoned. It's the willingness to swallow pain within a relationship. It's the terror of living without it. Men with women or men, women with either, with or without each other in any combination, we're on a dancefloor, in an arena of desire, on an enchanted island, trapped in merciless passion, rapt in slothful combat. In some dark Bloomsbury alley, on a November night, Tara holds on to Kim, stares at her like Hobbs at Wisnu or Andy. Kim hits her from behind. Tara survives, and takes her back. Hobb's death is an accident. If Alex kills him, they're always just miming the game of pain, the passion-play of love.

And as for me, I've been playing Hobbs' game ever since I came back from Bali. Buy, sell, barter, exchange. It doesn't matter, as long as I can keep Tara with me. And it's worn me out, worn me down. But she won't even hit me from behind. She doesn't care enough. Her occasional tendernesses are born of her own torment, or of boredom. Recognizing this I'm liberated, released from her. I've been clinging to ghosts, improvising love with shadows. There's no letting go I'll have to do. There's nothing to let go of. I don't have the courage to love any more. Maybe if I'd loved Lamia more, she'd have lived; maybe I haven't ever loved Tara, only desired her desire, her love of loving, and those were never mine. She's always said I'm compelled to leave the ones I love before they leave me, and she's probably right. Under profligate bougainvillaea, on a remote shore, a lost man grieves for Lamia, who eleven years after his defection revenged herself by not dying in his arms, and for Hobbs and for Tara, and even for poor wretched Alex who has the burden of a bludgeoning on his shoulders.

Leave others to grieve for their dead. Let me mourn my living as they leave, one by one, for their islands. The songs say that only death can break some bonds, but I should have learnt long ago that there are others life refuses early on to forge. Now I know that you can learn about the former kind when it's almost too late, and as for the latter, you can mistake them for the fated sort and be misled from milestone to near extermination before you know what's hit you. When I first knew Lamia was dying and began to grieve, that grief was for myself, for all those lost happenings and faces and things I hadn't admitted to. Then came the time of reckoning, the real death. And as for Tara, I think our meeting was a fluke throw in a game of chance, but I've kept wanting to find out the players' names, and what they thought they'd gain. Tara was saying, earlier, that I want to write destiny, write my own endings. Maybe that's what I've been doing, living an end to my stories.

Time up at the bar. We all might live in the same state, but I'm leaving. Let Kim take care of Tara and herself. The roulette tables and the gambling dens, the winter sales, the season of tawdry bargains – all over now, time to pack up the wares, send the remainders to a thrift shop, cut your losses, pay up and leave.

— Here's a poem for the moment.

Wreathed in clove-heavy smoke, I translate Faiz:

Stay by me/ My killer, my lover, stay by me/in the hour the night passes/laughing, dancing/jangling the violet anklets of pain . . .

— Don't be morbid, stop thinking about your friend.

— He wasn't my friend.

But I know she isn't talking about Hobbs. So I spend my last twenty pounds on champagne. But it's not destined, I soon find out, for the three of us or our farewell kisses. Kim wants to share it with the party. People are dancing on tables and chairs. Tara, my Balinese scarf in her hand, is doing something highstepping that looks like a flamenco. A freckled Irishman tries to follow her twisting steps. I'm tired. I want out. Then Kim takes the revolving Tara by the arm.

— We've got to go.

— Already? (That's me, hypocritical.)

— Oh, we've got another party to go to, didn't Tara tell you? (Kim turns to Tara.) Part of the deal, huhn? I said I'd come here with you if you came with me.

Doe-like, Tara's ready to leave. They ask if they should call me a cab; I should have known, when they brought their car, that I was to be dumped.

— We're not going your way, Sameer. (Kim)

— Can you lend me a fiver? You said you'd loan me a tenner if I went short for the bill. I'm not walking through the bloody west end at this time. (Me to Tara)

— I thought I'd brought more than I have. I've only got a twenty pound note left. I'll have to keep it for emergencies. There's a cashpoint at the corner, only a minute away. (Tara to me, with her love-to-help-you-but-I-can't-I-feel-so-guilty look)

Dully sober now, I see them to their jalopy. Another kiss, another caress. I shudder at my own falseness as I touch Kim's shoulder and kiss the air beside her cheek. Then, as I march into the Piccadilly night from the bank, I get pushed down from behind, by a gang of four, I think, or maybe I'm seeing double. They're muffled in black wool and leather. Mugged at knife point, smacked on the face and head, I aim a fist or a few before I go down flailing and fighting. My right arm takes my body's weight. My hand's numb, my lip sore.

I sit in a whitely lit cell, until the policemen remember I'm there. The big boys smell of beer, pig fat and vindaloo. They won't take me home in their van. But they want me to tell them what the boys who mugged me looked like. They keep pretending to write, even when I'm hesitant or quiet.

— Black, they must have been. Or Bangladeshi.

I want to reply: They weren't boys at all, the gang was led by two women called Kim and Tara. No, sorry, it was only Kim who mugged me and . . . but if it was Tara she mugged, where do I fit in, and what about Alex? And the angels all went off together in a jalopy when December told us it was dying. But now it's Hobnail that's dead, and I'm alive, or so I think . . .

But my tongue won't shape the words, my head's spinning from the fists and the fall, so I say:

— I'm sorry, there were three or four of them, boys they were, I don't know, about nineteen and all kinds of races, maybe there was a girl there too, the person who swiped my stuff when I was down was small, my back was to them and then I was too dazed – I'm wasting your time, all I wanted was some other poor bugger to be spared a few pounds and for you to take me home, I've still got my travel card, I can't help you and you can't help me so I'd best be on my way . . .

— We could get you an ambulance. You'd do better seeing to that hand of yours, mate, the cop tells me as I leave.

Seasons, buds, terror, the red rawness of me . . . On Piccadilly's pavements I sit down and bleed. I wrap my Balinese green scarf around my flayed left hand and watch the cotton's colour change. Another bloody year to swallow, I say, and laugh at the metaphor. I trace with my right forefinger the pictures my seeping blood paints: Tara's mouth plum dark with wine, Wisnu's wrists raised in the mudras of Solo, the grey-green eyes of Palestine, a sultry, whining sax, leather puppets, pavilions and the Leaning Tower of London, fish, hobnail boots enchained by violet anklets, Alex's rotten teeth, funeral pyres and obituary photographs, fruit that bears the salty tang of love. In her grave, Lamia's pale foot taps in time to the gamelan. Wild and earnest roses bloom high among Ubud's green leaves. Tara, my stained scarf tied sash-fashion around her waist, a frangipani behind her ear, is dancing. Behind her flits the gaudy butterfly troupe. She tosses her fatal roses up in the air to the singing of the lero-lero-lero and I wonder what colour my scar will be.

Sweet Rice

For Yasmien Abbasi,
who suggested a final, vital ingredient

A few weeks after her fortieth birthday (unremembered, unsung), Shireen underwent a brief crisis and then received an unexpected gift. This is how it happened:

Jamil, her husband – one of those dedicated bankers who spent his life between his office, his associates, his business trips and his bed – announced to her one Sunday from the shallows of early morning sleep that he had important people visiting from abroad and others to whom he desperately owed a seasonal invitation. In short, she had to cater for more than a dozen guests at less than a week's notice. The dinner, Shireen grumbled silently as she lowered herself deeper into the depths of Capricornian gloom, was to be next Saturday; and she knew she would have to excel herself, for even her best was never good enough for Jamil's Libran discernment.

And so it had always been. In this impossibly difficult city of London where even a powerfully-situated husband did not guarantee a work permit or a job for a doctor with a third world (read by the British as third class) degree and experience, her medical expertise – so many years, and so much of her widowed mother's savings spent on it – had been displaced to an ongoing culinary struggle to keep her husband tied to her table, with sundry colleagues (for deals meant more to him than domesticity) in tow.

Such was life. Take Timur – now seven, and growing away from his mother – to school; do the shopping at Safeway and Marks and Spencers on Edgware Road; go to Marylebone library for some Han Suyin books in which other Asian lands far from her own were reflected in a doctor's eyes; come home and desultorily clean up. (She'd dispensed with the idea of an au pair a while ago, for she needed something besides shopping to fill up the time that reminded her of the globe of her days which was filling up with sand, taking her further and further away from any chance of regaining her fine hospital job in Karachi. Or, indeed, of adding to her qualifications the required British degrees; Jamil had always found some excuse, saying Timur was too little and medical training here expensive, and then he didn't know how long this English stay, sojourn for her and idyll for him, was going to last. If Shireen asked him for what she called a time-table – 'How long will we be here, when will we go back? My job isn't going to wait forever, you know' – he'd respond, 'Don't be silly, you have to understand the New Economics; professionals like us don't have front doors in one place any more.' She didn't know whether to be insulted at his negation of her profession, or flattered by his inclusion of her in his. And now a Malaysian woman, who'd soon become more a friend than a cleaner, came in once a week to do what Jamil called the heavy jobs).

Then she'd cook for Jamil and his guests as well, for this, too, she insisted upon. But lately he'd suggested they order food from one of the fancy Pakistani lady caterers who were now proliferating in London, because once she'd said in irritation that she hadn't been brought up to cook for armies when he sprung a dinner for six on her. And now he thought her home cooking wasn't quite fancy enough for his guests though he thrived on it himself. But she wasn't going to subscribe to his theory of two weights and two measures – more than good enough for him but not for outsiders – and refused even to consider food from elsewhere. This, he claimed in contradiction to his earlier protests about her elitist disdain for polite feminine values, was due to what he called her elemsee upbringing . . . And once she'd seen a poster for an orchestra called LMC and wondered aloud why an orchestra would name itself Lower Middle Class until her friend Yasmien with whom she was walking down High Street Kensington shoved her in the ribs and said 'No, silly, that's a typically Pakistani term, LMC stands for the London Musician's Collective' . . . one did still laugh with one's friends sometimes. Usually, though, when Jamil wasn't here. And that was more and more often. Then she'd follow her daily routine with the addition of a visit or a walk with one of her two close friends, and come home and still persist in cooking, against modern dietary prescriptions, the dishes she loved like spinach with meat or potatoes, oil-rich courgettes and aubergines, rich buttery breads and dry, fragrant pea-speckled rice tinted yellow. Since that was the role she'd been allotted by life's scene-shifters, she'd be a housewife with all the perfectionism of her medical training. But all too often she couldn't eat alone, and her friends were occupied with their matrimonial tasks, so she'd freeze the food for some day when it rained or snowed. Then, in her favourite armchair, late into the night, she'd read and reread the stories of Han Suyin's life among the women of China and Malaya.

Now, this party. This time most of the expected guests would be associates or prospective clients from Asia-Pacific and the Americas. Monday today; Jamil had gone off to Brussels earlier this morning, flying from the City Airport which he found most convenient for flights to Europe (but all too often it was to the Asia-Pacific region he went, for that, he said, was where the economy was booming, and other Asians, too, should make sure of their slice of the cake.) Though Shireen dreaded his guests, with their wives who looked suspiciously at the clothes she'd had sent to her from Pakistan and snooped around her fixtures and fittings, she was determined to prepare something really special, and outdo those society hostesses whose homes he dragged her to every sixth week or so when he was here. She'd already run through her repertoire of homely fare; after all, as a medical student and then a practitioner, she'd hardly had time to acquire the skills of her family's women; some passive knowledge, some pragmatic tips and some inherited skills had so far sufficed. But now, with the frustrated and frustrating perfectionism that constantly chilled her bones, she wanted to cross the final boundary and cook one of the feasts she'd heard her grandmother describe with such chop-licking ecstasy.

Sweet rice. A delicacy remembered from the day she'd kept all her Ramzan fasts for the first time. Not the insipid sweet yellow stuff speckled with shaved nuts, but something lush and golden orange, laden with succulent pieces of chicken and ripe with the subtle and suggestive perfume of fruit. Grandmother had made it for her and named it – or so, in her eight year old's arrogance, she'd imagined – after her. Shireen pulao. Sweet rice.

Shireen's father was from Multan, but her mother's parents – as they'd loved to remind her – had come from some town in what were now the United Provinces in Northern India. They'd settled in Lahore many years before Partition, but retained the gentle gestures, the sweet tongues and the richly aromatic cooking of another era, another land. After 1947 the landholdings that had given them a small revenue and some claim to feudal graces had vanished; and unlike many others, they'd never applied for recompense, which would have been a futile endeavour, as those who complained of properties lost were so many and there just didn't seem to be enough to go around. Her grandfather had lived all his life on his physician's earnings, and her father, too, was a doctor; simple people, who'd fallen in a world that continued to respect material manifestations of heritage, but hardly elemsee as Jamil put it. That term, she thought in catty moods, suited him better; and what was worse, his family had the mentality of shopkeepers with new money. But that was the way things were these days in Pakistan . . .

Enough reminiscing for now, she thought as she turned the corner from Seymour Place into York Street, which led her home. (Above her, the inverted grey tin bowl of sky.) Grandmother was no longer there, and Mother had probably long since forgotten a recipe of such absurdly luxurious pretensions. Now where could she find it? Hardly any chance of recovering it from the exercise books filled up with recipes her mother had copied out in her arthritic hand, or Shireen had painstakingly translated or transcribed – her Urdu, so fluent when she was younger, had grown almost rusty from years of disuse. (Medical textbooks in Urdu? Don't make me laugh. They're written in untranslatable gibberish.) Then there were the volumes of Madhur Jaffrey cookbooks that Jamil had brought for her, probably as a burdensome hint – they'd been placed by her on a corridor shelf, proudly forgotten; though friends had told her the recipes within them were authentic, timesaving and good, the vanity of a good daughter, rich in the dowry of a thousand recipes tested and proved, forbade her from turning to them. Once upstairs, in the comfortable sitting room of her flat, feet tucked up beneath her in a favourite pudgy armchair, she swallowed her lumpy, irksome pride; a pile of discarded notebooks beside her, she inspected Jaffrey's tomes as if in search of some obscure remedy in a respected encyclopaedia. But to no avail. What would she do? Her goat-like determination refused to allow her to give up.

Sweet rice. It would have been a gesture so grand, so uncharacteristically flamboyant, a celebration of her home, and above all a defiant signature (named after her, the sweet rice, the indulgent grandmother had deceitfully said, the indulged child had gullibly believed) . . . What have I ever signed with a flourish, Shireen said to herself, do I even remember my signature? And this son of mine is his father's child, an English child, who prefers dubiously prepared hamburgers and chips fried in the greasy remains of God knows what forbidden animal to his mother's wholesome cooking, give him a fresh, sweet lassi and he asks for an artificially flavoured yoghurt . . .

Then a picture teased her visual memory. She went to the hall cupboard – in use this season, as their coats and winter things were stored there – and retrieved a chest in which some ancient objects of sentimental value (don't look back and above all don't smell or sniff, it only takes you to places surrendered) were stored. She knelt there on the carpet, rummaging, foraging. A red scarf. Two saris. And the bundle of books. They tumbled out – Perveen Shakir's first two volumes of verse, the single working woman's inspiration of her twenties. Those novels of A. R. Khatun that had delighted her between the ages of twelve and fifteen. ('Chaste, pragmatic romances', as a Frontier Post columnist, Shahnaz Aijazuddin – who'd recently written about the creative apathy of Western-educated Pakistani women, too – had described them, in a fulsome tone that amazed her because, as a teenager, she'd finally, regretfully relegated them to a corner, submitting to the senior schoolchild's unwritten law of westernization which decreed that anything local or ethnic, except the odd piece of mystic music, was suspect, unworthy, elemsee, while English was chic and desirable.) Then, some romances of Islam and of colonialism and the '57 uprising by Abdul Halim Sharar, whom the Urdu scholars of today considered as dated as Rider Haggard. Here, now. The classic book of recipes she'd been searching for. She'd taken the bundle of books from her grandmother's cupboard when the old lady died, aged eighty three; a sentimental gesture, followed by the contradictory, even furtive, action of hiding them, once she'd carted them to London, under piles of gauzy unusable garments behind her husband's sports gear and her son's array of sundry school things. A moth-eaten, mildewed book. The Urdu script was old-fashionedly pure and clear, faint now with time but still legible. On the frontispiece, under the title, the year of publication – 1911. *Naimatkhana*, the book was called . . . the traditional larder. She had never, when she took it away, imagined she'd have use for it in these labour-saving days and even the names, weights and terms in it, as she browsed, were archaic. But after a false and disappointing start, since it wasn't included in the book's list of contents, and she couldn't locate a familiar heading, the recipe appeared. On page 89. Orange rice, the author had called it. Chicken or lamb, rice, clarified butter, onions, coriander, garlic, salt, cummin, black pepper, cloves, cardamom and sugar. And then, for the remembered fragrance (heady, like playing the circle game with your favourite boy cousin in the sun), she had to turn to recipe no. 249, on page 192. A sauce of orange peel, almonds, pistachios, cardamoms, water and – for the final, special, touch – crystallized rock sugar. All ingredients so easy to find nowadays, in this city with no cuisine of its own to boast of; which had, in its usual, grudging and offhand way, taken to guzzling the delicacies of its erstwhile empire and was even developing an increasingly discerning palate for them. Little Asias of restaurants and eating places had taken over the city – the revenge of the spice islands, as she and Yasmien jokingly said when they chose places to shop and eat. The rock sugar, perhaps, would be difficult to locate – but Drummond Street, for a sturdy walker like her (she walked for hours in post-autumnal, leaf-bare Regents Park some-times) was only a short walk away, though she hated its dinginess and its stalely spicy smells. And if not, then Harrods or Fortnums would be sure to stock it . . . In the end, she'd have gone even beyond the remembered delight to create something new, something lavish and wonderful, a festive concoction that bore her name . . .

Later, though. For now she had found a companion. (Jamil always said, when he saw the increasing pile, in her usually orderly surroundings, of medical digests and newspapers, imported Heralds, Shes, and Frontier Posts, free handouts, Big Issues, and mail order catalogues she saved because there was always something she wanted to read again, that Shireen would even find something to devour with her eyes on the back of a cereal pack, an airline ticket or a postage stamp. It was a joke she was sure he'd picked up from one of the American men's magazines that were his only leisure reading, or from an in-flight journal, this tasteless description of the kind of passionate, indefatigable reader she was). The book would keep her engrossed, amused, transported, for hours.

When she reached the last of the recipes (homesickness sometimes is closer than anything to happiness), she still had half an hour before she left to pick up Timur, who she'd remembered had football practice after classes today, from his school near Marble Arch. She discovered an index of recipes at the end of the book; no point now regretting that she hadn't located it earlier, for half the fun of finding the recipe for sweet rice had been the search for it. Beyond the index was a list of books published by the same house. She realized that they were all by the author of this book, whom she'd imagined as a semi-literate bourgeoise, a turn-of-the-century housewife. Her ignorance astonished her – this woman, Muhammadi Begum, had been the editor of the first influential Urdu journal for women, which her husband had founded in Lahore in 1898. She had written at least a dozen books in the span of just ten years. Some were guides to housekeeping and good manners, but the titles of others, and the short, pithy blurbs below, made Shireen long for a grand library. A book for children: a young girl seeks a magic fountain, tree and bird to free her brothers, who have turned to stone, from captivity. (Will Jamil, too, free his limbs one day, from their pervasive torpor?) A tale for adolescents: a poor but highly learned young girl works day and night, setting up a school for girls, using her intelligence and wits to pay for her brothers' education and her mother's recovery from mental illness. (And here I complain, listless.) Two novels for adults: one about the evils of forcing an educated young woman – interested in the study of medicine and the art of herbalism – to marry her incompetent, dissipated cousin, and driving her to despair and death. (And what have I done? Jamil was not my cousin, but I didn't love him, and settled for a marriage of convenience because my work didn't give me time and I was afraid and over thirty.) A biography: of a role-model, an impoverished widow who'd become the principal of a vernacular girls's school in colonial Lahore, well over a century ago.

Muhammadi Begum. Who was she then, this master cook who'd stirred the ingredients of romance and realism into platters of parables that had nurtured generations of women, secluded or newly emergent from the confines of four walls and veils, adding a special prescription for those women who, almost a century later, were doctors and lawyers and opposition leaders and even prime ministers? Dead – so the prefaces, written by her stepdaughter and stepdaughter-in-law told Shireen – in 1908 at the age of thirty (and I am already forty, and still alive, and have abandoned my years of useful training and service to languish and moan in a luxurious central London flat), finding time to leave behind this keepsake of herself, this cookery book, the only work for which she was remembered, by a multitude of women who continued to share her bounty (and sharing bread is the closest form of love), taken from this *naimatkhana* she left behind her.

Naimatkhana. Simply translated, a larder or storehouse. Literally, a house or chamber of bounty. And it was from this chamber of bounty or blessings that Shireen would draw sustenance. She would share what she had, give unstintingly, take what was offered, laid out out on the *dastarkhan*, the fresh white banqueting cloth of life. All the way to Timur's school, she pondered, she brooded. Yes, the dish that bore her own name, that she would prepare; but she'd do much more. She'd go to the India Office library and excavate, reclaim whichever of Muhammadi Begum's writings she could find; she'd spend her remaining fallow years in this foreign country recreating a forgotten time from her own past, giving back to this amazing woman – of whom no photograph existed since, as a traditional Muslim woman, she had never forsaken her purdah – her purloined history.

On her way home, holding Timur's unwilling hand in the bus (like his father, her son didn't like to walk), Shireen paid little attention to the child's customary pampered nonsense. Streams of history flowed in her head. Like Shireen's own father, Muhammadi Begum's husband Mumtaz Ali had encouraged her endeavours – a radical religious scholar, Mumtaz Ali was a fighter for the rights of women to choose their own destinies, to emerge into the light of education and the dignity of unveiling, to marry and to divorce whom they chose, to walk and work in the world as men's equals. Recognizing her superior talent, he had set up a press for his youthful bride, published her books, and kept them and her memory alive for many, many years after her death . . . (and will Jamil think of me when I go? Or has living abroad pushed him back into some realm of the colonized, the spineless, who fear the vocal freedom of their equals and partners, as the ruler fears the mocking songs of his subjects? Does this city allow freedom only to those that fill its treasuries with borrowed or stolen pounds? And who will support me if I spend years researching the life of a woman whose potent writings are probably interred, by a trick of history and idle conservation, in the mildewed and mite-infested coffers of empire?)

Shireen had decided. When she'd finally settled Timur in front of one of his interminable Mario games – a special favour, on a weekday – she picked up the phone and dialled Yasmien's number. Yasmien's machine switched itself on. Resignedly, Shireen said: 'Call me when you can, it's nothing important . . . Well, actually, I wondered if you and your husband are free on Saturday, for dinner . . .'

'My husband's not here,' Yasmien's voice interrupted her, 'and I'm free all week. Sorry about the machine. I was avoiding Tehmina, you know how long she goes on . . .'

'Listen, I'm thinking of compiling a recipe book. You know, based on those recipes from our grandmothers' time? I'm thinking of calling it Sweet Rice.'

Half an hour later (or maybe two hours, for she hadn't looked at her watch when she called Yasmien, and they'd traversed a century and more in their conversation) she had a collaborator, a fellow conspirator. Yasmien knew of someone who knew a publisher in Pakistan, who may be interested in assisting Shireen in her project of writing about her new heroine's life. With the fashionable status of Asian food in Britain, they'd have no major problem in finding an outlet here for Sweet Rice. The fancy Pakistani lady caterers, once they'd wept their kohl in streams down their faces, would throng to the spectacular launch, and afterwards claim that the recipes they'd copy had originated in their mothers' kitchens. And Yasmien had suggested a subtitle, and a vital ingredient for their Bountiful Feast: there'd be lots of bright illustrations, and between the recipes, to refresh the palate like cool sweet water, they'd serve whatever stories they could uncover of the life of Muhammadi Begum, and as condiments they could recount their own experiences of living and cooking at home and in alien lands.

The Keeper of the Shrine

Shaheen Khan led his horse to the water, but it didn't want to drink. He left it to graze in the long sun-dried grass and went to wash in the river. The sky had been heavy with heat – and the air with dust – for days; the trees and huts across the river were hazy. His clothes were damp and his skin clammy with afternoon sweat. He splashed his face and his hair with sweetish brown water but found no relief. He took off his shirt and his shoes, set them down on the bank, rolled up his trouser legs and stepped into the river. He waded in knee-deep, bending now and again to splash his face, chest and back, or wet his hands.

Then he saw her.

She, too, had stopped to wash; set down her two brass pots, loosened her braid about her shoulders, and unfastened the neck of her shirt. She was thigh-deep in water, her head thrown back, her eyes closed. Her reflection rippled on the waves, and he thought she was an apparition, or a picture painted on the clouds by an angel, but he heard, as he approached, the tinkling of her silver ornaments, and knew she was there, and real. Then she heard him: some sudden sound or move he made disturbed her. Transfixed for an instant, like a scared forest creature, she stared at him, started, then pulled her scarf across her face and shoulders and ran. She had forgotten her pots. He waded across to the bank, but she was already far away. He ran, water dripping from his drenched trousers, with her heavy pots, one beneath his arm, one upon his shoulder. Listen, wait, he called, but she wouldn't stop, and then she did. Not knowing what to say, he said: Don't be afraid; only that.

Shaheen Khan was not yet twenty. He was the only son of the biggest landlord of the region. He had been sent away to study as a child, far from his home, which villagers called the fort – a maze of three-storied houses, cottages, stables, stores and tents, some buildings of reddish stones and others of mudbrick daubed white with lime. He had been to college in the city of Lahore. He was the first of his family to leave the village; his forebears had sometimes gone into the ravines to hunt, or made an expedition to a neighbouring village on a mission of revenge, to settle a dispute between peasants, or simply to indulge in some lighthearted banditry. He was of a different cut. But upon his return to this simple life – so far from that city where tall domes rose in gilded marble pride to converse with the skies and ruddy-faced English officials rode by in iron carriages that went without horses and you could see grey figures silently flicker on canvas screens at the bioscope – he realized that the sleepy life of the village suited him far better than the speed of his student days. He read poetry or history, rode out to the river and the edges of the ravine; shot rabbits, waterfowl or deer, but even more often, carried charcoal and a large drawing pad to draw pictures of the life around him which he would later elaborate in colour on canvas.

She didn't speak to him that first day. But the next day, and the day that followed, he went again across the fields to the river and waited for her. He would sit under a tree and watch her, as she came with her pots. Shame or modesty stopped him from approaching her, and he concealed himself from her, quickly sketching her movements in charcoal on sheets of white paper he'd brought for the purpose. It was she who spoke to him first.

You have taken my soul away, she said, by capturing my image on paper, and on judgment day the Lord will ask you to breathe life into it and I will have to surrender my spirit to this reflection of mine.

He knew she was only partly in earnest.

Whose daughter are you? he asked.

My name is Savera, she said, because I was born as the sun rose.

And as the days went by she sat with him for a half-hour at a time as he drew pictures of her and she told him her story.

My father lived in a village some miles away from here, and my husband is the money lender in this village. He was a widower with two sons and a daughter. He was rich, they said, and had already divided his fields between his sons. What remained was his. It would all be mine, he vowed to my father, if I became his bride. He took me away from my home and my parent's love when I was fourteen. He'd seen me at a wedding and begun to want me. When Badshah came to ask for me, my father thought he wanted me as a bride for his son who didn't have a son, and said he'd never give me away as a second wife. Then Badshah told him: I want her for myself. You can take back your fields and your house and forget the money you owe me if you let me have her. My father was enraged. He was proud, I was pretty, and he loved me so much. Like a wild horse, with fire in his eyes and smoke around him, he reared: We are poor, he said, but you can't make a mockery of me, I won't barter with you or trade my daughter for land or gold. Leave this house and don't come back.

The persecutions began some days later. Now a field caught fire, now my mother was chased and bullied on the road or my small brothers pelted with stones. Then my father was set upon and beaten. My sisters and I were forbidden to leave the house, even to fetch water. My father took a complaint to the village headman. Nothing could be done to protect him, they told him, he was a debtor. Badshah was a powerful man, and beyond the headman's jurisdiction. Then my father caught fire. No one knew how it happened, but many saw him, walking through the village with his clothes and his flesh on fire. He reached our doorstep. God's hand, they said, was on his head; he was a pious man, God-fearing. When he called on the Lord to help him, the Lord brought him home. But I ask: If the Lord was there to bring this burning man home, where had he gone when they set fire to him? Where was he when Badshah's sons came to claim me; when my mother, her eyes half-blind with weeping, wrapped me up in her red wedding veil, hung a hoop in my nostril and sent me away with our tormentor?

I remembered my father's words: Badshah killed me, he'd said. Sometimes, when I lie by the old jackal at night, I want to kill him, strangle him with my scarf or stick one of his own knives between his ribs. Or poison his food. But I'm fearful. For my mother and sisters and small brothers. He'll set his thugs on them, as he did with my father. Lord, my life is hell on this earth; a long, damp, slow-burning night, only beyond the grave will I see daylight. If I hadn't seen your face I'd have been in the dark for ever.

With her red-and-yellow veil grazing her golden cheek and her teeth flashing like knives, Savera was as beautiful as a ripening fruit and as bright as a small silver dagger. She was nearly as tall as Shaheen, with a proud small head, golden eyes, a straight, supple back and taut high breasts. Tacitly, Shaheen knew when they first began to speak that their meetings would continue. He waited for her, and she came. Sometimes, she said, the women asked her why she'd started getting back so late. She'd cross the river, drenching her skirt to the thighs, and when she walked by them the women called her brazen for bathing herself under an open sky, and revealing her limbs in clinging, damp clothes. I fell into the water, she'd say with a laugh. She had a bold, laughing nature, which her husband hadn't broken, though he'd tried and kept on trying.

I don't even know your name,
stranger, and I've become yours.
I lie in your arms and the sun pours
sweet honey on us. Look! The mustard

blossoms are little torches we've lit
with our fires. My skin's turning
as dark as yours with the heat of your
arms. My face burns day and night.
In my sleep my feet twitch and the song
of my anklets wakes me up. I yearn
to find you, to run to you. I'm yours
like the wanton I am with you.

Are you from another village, she asked him, you have a strange
manner of speaking, your accent is not ours. What is this strange garb
you wear? Trousers so narrow and your shirt tucked in at the waist
and a broad leather belt? No cap, no moustache, your skin soft like a
girl's? Are you a wanderer, a soldier, a thief? I know nothing about
you. In response he lied and told her stories. She laughed, mocked
him, let him hide his rank, his name. Then one day he told her: his
father had a hundred villages, was the region's most powerful man.

He is a just man, Shaheen said. And good, if somewhat stern. I will
go to him and ask that justice be done. To order your husband, who
took you against your will, to release you. And when Badshah lets you
go I'll take you up the hill to the fort as my bride.

She put his finger to his lip.

You are hot-headed, too young, too rash. If it were true, if it could
be, I'd live with you as your hidden whore. But it will never happen.
Unless you take me away, from here, for ever. He'll never let me go.
He'll find me and kill me.

We'll go to the big city then. Where no one can find us. I'll get a job
in a big office. Work for the white-skinned men.

Shaheen's father called him to tell him that Badshah had lodged a
complaint against him for seducing his wife.

Stop this madness, he said, or I'll send you far away from here.
You'll never see her again. I'll send you to the army. Or flog you with
my hands.

Shaheen screamed, pleaded, protested. He wasn't yet twenty, and his blood was as hot as the riverbank on a summer day. And then, to buy time and keep peace, he promised.

But he couldn't sit still. Somehow they met again. The sun shining on fields of yellow and on the green river. The wild geese flying down from the white cloudless sky, spreading their white wings, calling in the tall grass. His charcoal and his drawing pad stolen as they lie wrapped in each other's arms and sleep. A second wind of caution and then the dark clouds and the rain like silver arrows and Savera draped in her heavy black veil like a city woman and Shaheen dressed like a villager again as they leave. He pulls her up in his arms and seats her in front of him on the horse's back. They have taken nothing – neither of them – from their homes. They say their goodbyes in a long silent moment, he to his father's soil, she to the fields where she lived in hell until she met her hot lover.

He saw us. He saw me half-naked in your
arms. He followed me. I was foolish and had
lost shame. I stayed with you longer each day.
His own daughters-in-law mocked him when they
saw me return late to the village. Ember-red
with loving. He followed me. He wasn't brave
enough to challenge you there and then.
He knew you always carried your gun and you'd
kill him in that remote place. The villagers
know you're rash. You'd have killed him
and borne the consequences. No, he meant to
touch your father's honour and pride
and his sense of village justice.

They were fugitives for two nights. And then apprehended as they lay sleeping in a field. A sudden cold night in the heat: fireflies flashing here and there. Badshah came with his sons, and uniformed policemen from the nearest town: mercenaries hired for this hunting expedition, a battalion to track down a sole wounded beast, with an armoured car like a tank. Savera and Shaheen dirty and exhausted and starving. They tried, both of them, to fight: she gave up first, but not without kneeing some of them in the groin and scratching their faces with her strong nails. They grabbed her by the hair, by the wrists; trussed her up, like a doe, in ropes torn from her own shawl. Shaheen kept on fighting, as he watched his lover surrender, but they bested him. They had stolen his gun from him as he lay asleep. He had no other weapon, not even a knife, and they were fully armed. Badshah's band dragged Savera away. The policemen, it transpired, had been sent by Shaheen's father. They shot his horse while he watched; they handcuffed him, and drove him home.

When Shaheen was brought home in handcuffs, his father was mute. It was only later that Shaheen came to know: when Badshah had come again to lodge a second complaint – bringing with him the pictures he had drawn of his naked wife, Savera – and Shaheen had already been missed – his father had given permission to have the errant lovers hunted down and brought home, sending along the police escort to ensure Shaheen's safety and avoid the possibility of an 'accident'. Savera's punishment was in her husband's hands. By the law of the region, an adulteress was allowed to escape alive, with her nose slashed and her braid lopped off. Some clans stoned adulterous couples to death. Flogging guilty males was recommended in Shaheen's clan, for a precedent to be set in the village, but so scandalously flagrant an affair had not taken place in their family in in common memory. Shaheen's punishment was outside the bounds of secular law and could only by administered by his father's hand.

My son has been bewitched. He's the victim
of a whore's stratagems. I'll flog him myself,
in public, but that won't cure him. I'll send

for doctors from Lahore, even from Delhi, to put
his head right. She's given him menstrual blood
to drink. She's driven him crazy. He's under her
spell, my poor reckless son.

Shaheen's father took a lash to him: not in public, but in the presence
of the most trusted members of the clan. Badshah's sons were also
there, and the village elders who would narrate the story, over the
communal evening pipe, in the village square. As a scholar of ancient
edicts, the landowner knew that the whip had only to graze the lad's
skin and draw blood just once. Shaheen's flesh was almost unmarked,
but his entrails and his eyes dripped with silent blood. He lashed out
at his father, calling out, over and again, his lover's name. They
strapped him in a straitjacket and took him away. The doctors from
Lahore were in attendance. How strange, he thought, as they fed him
powders and made him down potions, that he'd once planned to enrol
for pre-medical studies until the thought of cutting up cadavers had
made him take up draughtsmanship instead.

Shaheen slept for some days without dreaming. Or sometimes his
dreams were strange, wild, clawing at his skin like flying lynxes,
beating around his head with the greyish wings of cannibal bats. They
watched him night and day. The fine chains kept him bound.

Days of slow-burning darkness, daylight only beyond the grave.

Where have they hidden you, Savera, where
have you gone, have they whipped you, branded
you, broken your skin? Come carve with your
nails the new red flowers from my flesh. Wake
me from my death. I scream like a fallen bull-
elephant. I sleep on a bed of nails. I am an empty
cage, an unlit pyre or an unmarked grave. I am a
dirge for an absent corpse. So many nights I bleed
away, still singing.

When he rose, he began to paint portraits of her; but her features had become faint. He created hazy images, incomplete: eyes and mouth and enlarged nipples only, or faceless torso without hands, or a faint white form kneeling in the green river of grass, abject in prayer or supplication. Savera wasn't really in these pictures at all, her memory an abstraction. On his canvas there were faint blurred forms of blue, grey, pale yellow and white. They thought he was cured or over the worst and now they let him sleep alone.

And then she woke him up one night: breathed softly on his cheek. She was fragile, worn, her skin pallid, but she was beautiful. His head was heavy with the opiates they still gave him and he wondered if he was dreaming. She lay down beside him and her sweet smell was almost swallowed by the smell of abandon as if she'd been kept prisoner in a closed room for days. Her white clothes were dingy and her breath smelt of hunger. But he wanted all of her. She silenced him when he spoke but, seeing his exigence, began to make love to him. He fell asleep, exhausted, in her arms. When he awoke she'd left but the strange, new smell she bore. That scent of dust, incense and enclosed spaces surrounded him, it was on his skin and on his sheets.

Two nights passed and she was there again beside him. How had she managed to escape the vigilance of the watchmen and the servants to enter the house and his room? Was this an opium dream, a waking fantasy: seeing her, touching her, feeling her, entering her secret places? Was it a reward, for the terrors they'd shared?

She took his hands and kissed them finger by finger, then gave him her fingers to kiss. Her palms and nails were stained with henna. He was sweating, drenched in need, riddled with desire. Stay with me, Savera, he says, or take me with you, and she replies, I must leave as morning breaks. You must not follow me. But on Saturday, if you can escape, you must go to Badshah's house and call him out in my name. When he comes you must set fire to him, as he did to my father. No one will see you. I swear. I will drug the food and water his sons take in the evening, they'll be dead to the world. Then you must set fire to his house and come to wait for me by the wall of the old shrine on the hill. Do not enter the shrine at any cost. Keep silent, whatever you see. You must not speak or move until I call for you.

The doctors had said Shaheen was cured. But nothing had changed. He was still ready, if she would only reveal her hiding place, to go to Savera: escape with her, since their world wouldn't allow them to live together in peace, forgetting language, region and even faith if they must. He still came out in cold sweats and rashes when he thought of her return.

He managed, on Saturday night, to escape; strangely, the world seemed to be sleeping. At the threshold of Badshah's homestead, he called out his name: Come out, moneylender, he said, in your wife's name. Badshah emerged. Shaheen slapped him three times on the face before he stabbed him in the side. And while Badshah was still breathing Shaheen set fire to his shirt. Then, flinging kerosene on the doorstep, he set that, too, alight. Shaheen left Badshah screaming, but there was no one to rescue him and the night fell as thick and heavy as tar.

Half a mile from his victim's house Shaheen vomited up a mess of bile and half-digested potions. Months of medication and seclusion had made him feeble: and yet, he felt, he couldn't have done what he had tonight without the help of the opiates they'd been giving him. He had come out on foot, dressed like a local peasant, to avoid being recognized; in the darkness, it took him more than an hour to walk to the shrine, which wasn't a shrine at all but the ancient abandoned temple of some deity the villagers had long since forgotten. It was still thought to be inhabited by spirits and the villagers stayed clear of it.

Shaheen, wrapped in the grey shawl he'd brought against the night's chill talons, sat down by its northern wall, beside a slender pomegranate tree covered in fleshy red flowers. A sickle moon hung in the sky, like a dead beast's twisted horn. He waited in the thick, rank darkness for morning and for his lover who bore morning's name. Then he heard movements in the night. Three men arrived on horseback: he recognized the coarse tones of Badshah's second son. They have followed me to punish me for their father's death, he thought, now my time is near and I'll never see Savera again. But in spite of the light of the torches they lit, they didn't even look in his direction. The third and shortest of them went back to his horse, returning with a gunnysack. Get out, whore, he said, and shook the sack open. A woman fell out, her arms and legs trussed up, a bandage tied around her mouth. Shaheen had recognized the hideous, limping form of Badshah. Then who had he killed just a few hours before? And how had the drugged sons awakened from an opium stupor and escaped from a burning house? Had he merely dreamed what he'd done a few short hours ago? The woman they held captive was Savera – was it to see this that she had summoned him here? The men untied her and she screamed. Shaheen was caught in an invisible grip; he couldn't move. He watched as the men smashed his beloved's hands and then her feet with their clubs. We'll cut you to pieces, whore, the second son roared, and his father said: Enough, have mercy, just kill her now, and the elder son came at his stepmother the with a knife. As he rammed it into her ribs Shaheen's lost voice came back and screaming he struggled to rise. He saw the forms of Badshah and his sons dissolve into shadow before he fell into oblivion.

There was no sound nor movement around him when he awoke by the wall. The sun's first rays were trying to penetrate a smoky curtain of cloud. He rose. There was nothing left to do now but search for her. What they'd done to her corpse to disgrace her in death he didn't even begin to imagine. They must have hidden her in the abandoned temple. He walked in: now that she was dead, what use to obey her instructions, which had any way proved futile? The courtyard smelt of incense and disuse. He walked past the smashed image of a pagan deity. The earth in the inner courtyard was red with ancient stains, marks of the sacrifice of some beast, probably a goat. Then he found her or what was left of her. They had shaved her head and cut off her arms and her legs. The corpse was in a state of decay. He knew now that his waking dream had re-enacted the true events of her death. They'd smashed Savera's hands and feet before they killed her. But when? How long had she been there, how long after had he lain in bed, how many moons had waxed and waned since that night when they dragged her away, the night that was probably her last on earth? He recognized her silver ornaments and the talisman that hung round her neck. He gathered up her bones in his shawl and took them to the river where he scrubbed them clean till they shone like alabaster. He said the prayers for the dead and laid her polished bones to rest in the shade of the pomegranate tree.

When they came to find him, Shaheen had ceased to speak, but the villagers seemed to think he'd performed an act of heroism. The entire village had taken the blame for the burning of the hated moneylender and his homestead: his sins were so great that people didn't even object or pronounce the act a crime. It was known that Badshah's family had murdered Savera's father and then the girl herself. Badshah's sons had perished in the fire that destroyed his house; his sons-in-law sold their fields and left the village, with Badshah's wailing daughters, for ever. Shaheen's father, mortified and flooded with grief at the mishaps in which he'd carelessly played so great a part, put a bullet in his own temple. No blame was ever laid on Shaheen's head, but then they understood that he was crazed. He never travelled far from the shrine and his lover's grave. People would come to talk to him: they did not know whose grave it was that he tended with such ferocious ardour, but they knew it was a shrine to love, and soon the young of the village came to see Shaheen as a wise man or a holy fool, and the shrine he guarded as a sanctuary for the homeless and the unprotected. They said that the spirit of a murdered princess of days gone by lived in the pomegranate tree, and granted favours to star-crossed lovers. The mute saint was the keeper of her shrine. People came from distant villages to bring him offerings of food and fruit, and flowers for the grave; they waited on him while he bathed in the river. They would ask him questions and he would respond by tracing mysterious signs in the dust: very occasionally words, but more often pictures that told of the secret hopes and yearnings his questioners had failed to reveal. To make his mosaics he would go out into the forest, collecting herbs and the brittle wings of fallen insects to mix his paints and powders. So they brought him trays, buckets and baskets of coloured powders, and on certain days he would turn the dun earth around the shrine into a carnival of colour with his riotous and enigmatic pictures, only some of which made sense to the onlookers. He would leave the pictures intact for only hour or so; later, the earth itself would become variegated and multi-hued with the powdered dyes, and children would bring pails to collect the bright dust of the shrine for their games. It was thus, though, that he revealed, one day, the story of Savera: how she'd loved him and run away with him, how her husband had murdered her in the shrine; how she'd come back from the dead to find her lover, to demand revenge and the killing of her cruel master and re-enact before his eyes the true events of her death. Every one knew he'd been locked up, and drugged at the time, but they also knew something wondrous had happened to him that no one could adequately explain. They say he sat there for fifty years and more: and every now and then, someone would come to him to see the telling of the story, which he repeated every year on the anniversary of the night he'd discovered her remains. The next day he would wipe away the mosaic he'd so painstakingly composed. He died, on the anniversary of the night he'd first come here, at the age of seventy. He was found lying on her grave, by the day's first pilgrims, at the hour of sunrise which was when, it was said, he had laid her bones to rest. Many still live who saw him, and the day of her burial was adopted as a local feast, and so it remains, after his death. The flickering images of his romance and its travails had become part of local memory and his story was repeated from village to village. It is sung as a ballad by singers who come to the shrine each year, and sometimes performed on radio and television. And it makes a stirring tale to be told around bonfires on wintry nights, the legend of the passion of Shaheen and Savera, the unlawful love that lasted long, long beyond the grave.

Benedetta, Amata

Later, when they asked her, she would always say: I met him at a shared desk at university in 1978. It was true and it wasn't. Benedetta was in my Persian class and I noticed someone who looked about twelve years older than me. But it was a few days later when we were sitting in the vestibule eating our sandwiches, and I spoke to her in my easy Italian, that we got to know each other. Soon she told me I could address her with the informal *tu*. And then a mutual friend said I should look out for her but we were already friends. We started to study together at her house or mine and see esoteric films and we connected – because she was Italian, I loved Italy, she'd been to the East and more than that she was an expatriate and a polyglot like all my friends. At school we shared coffee and sandwiches. It took me a while to see that with her thin, strong body, her grey-blue-green cat eyes and her mass of red wavy hair she was quite beautiful. She was older than she looked, born twenty-four years before me, exactly old enough to be my mother as she'd later delight in telling me. Born in Italy to an American mother with Jewish and Irish blood and an aristocratic Italian father who was partly – he claimed a quarter – Red Indian. She'd been an actress, singer and dancer in the US; given it all up to return to Italy and marry. But homelessness – in a glamorous way – seemed to pursue her and there was an itinerant atmosphere around her marriage.

About a year after we met I told her I was a pillhead but I didn't say it quite that way because I didn't really know. What I did was sanctioned by my doctors, encouraged by them, had been for two years. First I'd been given diazepam to help me unwind and sleep when I was working in a thankless banking job. My parents were unworldly, perfectionist idealists who'd passed on to me their idealism and perfectionism. Some of that I'm proud of but sometimes it's a stranglehold, a noose. Added to that was a heritage of *noblesse oblige*. I was also an optimist and a dreamer. I'd gone to the bank because we'd found ourselves relocated in a milieu that dismissed and despised dreamers. And then, when the banking job made me work hard, well and fast during the day and go into a passable imitation of an epileptic at night, I saw my first therapist without actually knowing what he was because I connected therapy with psychiatry. He told me I should go back to studying and take some pills in the meanwhile to see me through the phases of transition.

After that I'd joined university, met B, combined my course with a part time job at an office for survival money as I didn't have a grant. And got violently depressed during my first long summer holiday. Everyone had gone away, I'd had another desultory affair, and I felt with reason that I was a failure at love. I didn't know what to do with myself except write in my journal. And take pills. So I'd gone to my GP and told him what I'd had before. After charging me 50p for some bizarre motive he'd put me on more antidepressants and some sleeping pills in case I needed them. And when B suddenly came back that summer I told her how depressed I'd been, how it made me feel I was crazy, how the medical men thought I had to be on medication to get through my days. B described herself as Mother Tiger and she'd handpicked me as one of her cubs. So I supposed her protective instincts would be aroused and help me face my unnamed, unrecognized enemy. I'd learnt from reading about depressed artists that madness and badness could be glamourized and though I didn't feel there was anything glamorous about the peculiar combination of the two that I'd been accused of, at least I'd found a tentative language to express my state. I was twenty four. Till then my pill-taking had been a silent, compulsive activity. I took pills to face people because I was feeling low, afraid, incompetent, inadequate. To feel fast when I was slow and slower when I was gaining too much speed.

Funny how people don't really think about or notice the things you do when you're alone. A drunken night in company might make your best friend tell you that you drink too much though with someone like me, they should know that if I'm on my own I never drink and one hangover is enough to make me sick at the sight of a drink for at least a week. Then again we forgive those around us for drinking too much, when we don't even notice the panic of a friend who's caught up in the slow, silent process of taking pills, because drugs don't have the loud stink of alcohol, which erases the solitude of drinking.

It was on the bank of the Little Venice canal near my house with the leaves of low-hanging branches heavy above our heads that I told B about my depressions and the pills. I thought she was only aware of the symptoms and not the solutions I'd found, but two years later when we were closer still, like two arms of one body, and my depressions and their cure were conflated, she said she'd noticed that sometimes when we'd gone together to the movies and on other occasions as well I'd been 'too relaxed'. By then she'd abandoned her degree and I'd finished mine.

Three months after I received the news of my upper second I didn't wake up one morning. I hadn't wanted to do anything serious, just not wake up. Yasmien, who'd rung me up late at night with a problem, had heard me sounding incoherent and wondered if I was drunk but she knew I wasn't much of a drinker so she called the flat again early in the morning. My sister, who was staying, was alerted and woke me up soon enough to stop the pills from doing any real damage. What I got for my gamble was the worst drug hangover I've ever had. I don't recommend even the lowest overdose of Mogadon to anyone as a cure for insomnia. Too much to pay as forfeit. You feel you're the living dead and your skin's so thin that you're like one big ear full of noise.

Funny. I should have been feeling quite high. I'd spent the summer in Italy, knowing unofficially I'd done quite well in my exams which meant that I'd probably be able to stay concealed in the hermit cells of academe as a doctoral candidate for another three years. There was every chance of a teaching career after that. I was in my mid-twenties, spoke several languages, and had a growing reputation as a folksinger. Much of my time in Rome was spent with musicians, performing, experimenting and recording tapes for radio broadcasts. I was considered attractive – probably because a combination of gifts, youth and a secret yearning to be wanted created a vulnerability around me which looked like sexual charisma. I'd play along but get terrified when anyone tried to get too close and seek for safety in numbers, causing chaos around me, rivalries I couldn't cope with, clichés I'd unwillingly compounded. Because I was convinced, and life had proved me right, that binding myself to one person would leave me bruised and betrayed in the end. Because even now the worst way to handle me is to try and manipulate or harangue me. I couldn't bear liars. I was – am – deeply timid. Terrified of crowds, of strangers. Once I remember during that time asking a lover I was begging to let go of me – because we just couldn't agree about anything – what it was that had made her want me and stay with me a whole summer. She said: As soon as I saw you I wanted you in bed and I still do. And I knew I'd done everything to please her and so many others who hadn't loved me before that and rarely felt fulfilled myself, only soiled, used and unloved in the end. That's why I'd learned to be the one to run before everything got too involved and complicated.

The future was so frightening that just thinking about it killed the present for me. I'd pop a couple of pills or tranquillizers though not in a way that would be noticed or make anyone say they were taking my life over. But Stefano, the friend whose room in Rome I was sharing, guessed what I did – he'd seen the animation turn to panic, nerves and feverishness and then the transition to chemically induced docility. He'd say: *Non prendere le pasticche. Non ti fa bene. Cerca dentro di te la forza di combattere la tua angoscia. Sei poeta. Non vendere la tua bellezza.* But if I was a poet the few lines I scribbled here and there, usually in letters or my diary, certainly didn't make me feel that my destiny lay in writing. Music was my breath, words were ephemeral. Once at the end of a hot July day we'd run away to the Ostia beach, seeking each other's silence out like men do together sometimes when they've had enough of erotic tension and of their lover having had enough of them. The sun was setting in a livid sky and the sea was melting platinum. I was putting on my act: writing verses on the sand to prove that all words like those were written only to be wiped out. Love, language, poetry, life and all that shit – eminently disposable. Stefano's was an earnest soul. His dogged and denied Catholicism blocked the way to the authentic Eastern mysticism he aspired to. (I'd met him a year before in London where I'd given him impromptu lessons in my language and culture. He'd discovered the tormented East in Mother Teresa's mission in Calcutta. I was a very different version of it.) He said: You're sad and you're making me sad. Sometimes I feel you are just too far away from me. And your friendship with that woman just isn't doing you any good. Of course he meant B, whose effortless elegance he admired and also envied. I used to talk to her often from Rome.

Stefano was a great believer in earthly pleasures, but also in self-mortification. He'd be vegetarian for weeks and abstemious and then go on great binges of eating every part of a pig he could lay his hands on, washing it all down with beer and red wine. Talk to me, talk to me, show me who you are, he'd say to me after a few glasses, and who the fuck knows why but I had tried. At the end of the summer I left him and Italy with a speech he'd made buzzing in my ears: You're a self-destroyer. You've ended up identifying with the myth of the *poeta maledetto* before becoming the poet you should be. I didn't know what the hell a damned poet was and certainly didn't want to be one though later when I read Baudelaire I thought of Stefano. He also said it was time for me to go back home. It was India he meant, it didn't matter that I came from military-ridden Pakistan, which I'd left aged thirteen. Bhutto had been sent to the gallows there just three years ago.

Stefano was on his way to the Ganges himself. He felt I'd lost something, left something behind. He said I had to go home and collect a fistful of my native soil as a talisman or I'd be lost. And when I saw her in London B seemed to parrot Stefano's words. I'd changed. She didn't know what I wanted any more, she couldn't reach me. *Parlami, parlami – dove sei?* I was taking out on her all the frustrations I'd built up but that was because she wouldn't let go of me, stood for my silences and absences and my unbearable angst and my talk of the distance of God. It was almost twelve years later, after B died and the grief I held in wouldn't go away, would burst and stifle and burst and stifle me again, and I'd tell myself I was mourning her so terribly because I felt so guilty and ashamed that I'd never loved her enough during my lifetime, that the truth came to me. It was in a diary of a trip we'd made together late in the summer before she died. (We've come full circle, she said: seen each other in all our continents. She'd forgotten her America.) I'd written: I'm here with the person I've loved almost more than anything in the world.

The language of grief – Lord, how do we find it, where does its blue flow? Hands, like birds, search the air but there isn't any air, the sky's gone or the horizon is black, they falter, the birds, they fall . . .

It took me two years to turn B's death and my love for her into a story and when I did it wasn't as if I was free of the loneliness that responded to her leaving, that I'll never be, but I knew I could write again without being ordered, it was what I had to do because she'd wanted me to, writing wasn't a cure or a surrogate for life or even a cleansing, it was often hateful and pain-laden instead, but it was a record, a remembrance, an unending attempt at reparation.

The birds of grief keep flying, they falter, they fall, they stutter and stammer and stumble . . .

But back then, in 1981, I had no words. Admitting that I loved Benedetta so much would have diverted me from the straight lines I so desperately wanted to follow. The words and demands of my intimates and my disappointment when a letter came telling me that my upper second and my thesis proposal just weren't good enough for a grant must have fed into my need for oblivion and for the pills I took that autumn night. The burden of dreams was too great for me. I was receiving guidelines from those I loved best and wishing they'd stop casting me as a lost wanderer from the exotic east but I'd begun to forget what 'me' was or wanted. So I went to India after eleven years of absence to bring back that fistful of soil and an answer for them. My grandmother's death earlier that year told me it was time to go back. After leaving Karachi for good and before moving on to England I'd spent nearly a year at thirteen travelling around Indian hotels and luxury homes with my father before settling down for eighteen months at a school in Ooty which unhinged me. So in many ways I knew India better than any other country though I'd always felt like a foreigner there except with my grandparents. But the return journey worked, in part. I was in Delhi, a city I didn't know at all, through November. In a garden full of parrots I regained myself, looked at my self-destructive urges and told them I didn't admit they existed.

Two years later, two years of unemployment or itinerant, unrewarding jobs, of throwing my body around in loveless love affairs, of letting myself be cheated by friends and putative employers, lacking the confidence to commit myself in words to anyone who might love me the way I wanted to be loved, I was openly chained to medication prescribed by Harley Street charlatans. They mistook my despair at my lack of success and direction for manic depressive symptoms and tied me to a course of treatment that I found humiliating. Strange: it was on B's recommendation that I went to the Harley Street shrink who put me on what he assured me was a wonder cure. I realized later that B sent me there as a kind of aversion therapy, because she thought I'd become too easily used to what she called the junk my GPs were giving me, pills to sleep and pills to wake up and pills to make the sun rise and go down. But my swings of mood from elation to despair to tranquillity were too tough for me to handle. I'd been brought up to prize equanimity and fortitude above all else, to show only calm surfaces to the world.

In autumn I travelled to Frascati to spend the weekend with a friend before meeting B in Rome. She'd moved back to Italy the spring before. She'd left me half-healed and pretending to be in love with someone new. I met her at a restaurant near the Spanish Steps. She told me: I can't take you home with me, your trip's been a waste, my husband has had bad news, he's in a state of stress, can't countenance the idea of an intruder. I could give you some money to make your holiday worthwhile. But I refused a handout. I'd worked all summer at an editorial hack job to save for the holiday. I took the next train back to Frascati, flushed all my pills down the loo, and never took them again. I apologized abruptly to the friend I was staying with and left by train for London via Paris less than twenty-four hours later.

I suppose I went through a series of silent withdrawal symptoms. To the few friends I hadn't asked to leave me alone I seemed calm or at least calmer. The agitations were hidden. I allowed B to make up with me, or at least to think she had. Bits of work started to come my way: research for documentaries, editorial work on coffee-table books by semi-academics, interviews, tentative moves towards a career in cultural criticism or the cinema or the nascent multicultural media. A friend suggested I use my degree and my bilingualism to translate the Urdu stories of her Uncle Manto into English. For some weeks I immersed myself in his underworld with its fumes of illicit moonshine and poverty but I couldn't stay there.

I had a lonely friend I'd met at B's house on one of her return trips, a violinist from Barcelona who couldn't speak English and couldn't find work. He languished in an attic while his English girlfriend went to college each day. He wanted me to write a series of poems he could set to music. I could perform them with and without other voices. Joan was a sort of reincarnation of Stefano, whose friendship was no longer a part of my life, since he felt I hadn't lived up to his ambitions for me and I'd got sick of his preachiness. Joan somehow also seemed to reflect back to me a younger version of myself in a dark mirror. He gave himself up to his moods and his creative urges with a savage self-indulgence and matched it with rigid discipline when it came to his music. He practised on his violin for hours in solitude in front of his reflected image, or wrote scores hunched up on the rug with a flowing wastepaper basket beside him. We'd walk in the park in the late winter of my twenty-ninth year and he'd make me speak the poems he thought would express my hidden talent to the world. Then I'd tell him pared-down accounts of my life story in exchange for his confessions and he'd go away and compose passages of music which he'd say I'd inspired. I'd tell him stories of what I described as near madness and he called frustrated creative expression. I set all my troubles in the past tense. I abandoned a symbolic epic he'd suggested to me and started trying to write again from zero. Finally something gave and I produced a series of poems – songs, really – all dedicated to Layla, the girl in Karachi I thought I loved. I never did send them to her so I don't think she ever really knew what I felt. Joan said they were too intricate and personal to set to music. Your own voice is the only music they need, he said. I've still got fragments of those musings in a file somewhere, unlooked at for years and unredeemable. The shavings left by an apprentice carpenter.

I spent my twenty-ninth birthday alone on a dune in a white desert near Jaisalmer. The moon was full and I was full of something new which I swore would never leave me, a fire that burned for everything and everyone, that I could bear as long as nothing touched me, as long as I could remain remote, inviolate. I'd discovered a new land: I'd never travelled so widely in Rajasthan before. But my mother's mother was born here and it laid claim to an atom of me. 'Its sands shine like hills of gold, its trees gleam like emeralds, the star of my eyes, my land' . . . Its songs still surface between some of the lines I write. The Pakistan border was a few miles away. I had planned to cross it as soon as I could. See Layla in Karachi. But circumstances or my own doubts about my fatherland stopped me in midflight. In London my younger sister gave birth that day to twin sons. I was making notes for poems, filling up my diary with impressions of my travels in this arid, beautiful land.

A month later, from London, I rang up Layla in Pakistan. She told me it was no good, our chances had been few and were over. I realized again that the burden of my dreams was too much for me. I was in emotional exile and home was at best a temporary spot but more often the land where I was not. It was May. I reached for some sleeping pills left behind in one of my early secret caches and began to pop them like peanuts. When they wouldn't work I got hold of a bottle of something – gin, I think – to wash them down with, which I hadn't done before, but I hated myself so much that I wanted to do hideous and debased things I wasn't meant to do. I didn't like the face I saw in the mirror so I grabbed a disposable Bic razor from the dresser and started to sketch signs on my forehead. It was early morning and the sky had begun to pale, become a sick violet. Then I got to work on my wrists. I didn't really like the sight of my blood on the sheets but I don't think it was death I was looking for, just a long, long sleep. And it wasn't me I was attacking but the snakes that lived in me, jumped out and stung just when I was in peace or in oblivion, the snake of my tongue that twisted and betrayed me, the snake of my past . . . The phone rang and went on ringing. I had to stop the sound. I rose and picked up the receiver from its cradle. Those ten steps were enough to make me pass out. I remember Joan's face in the ambulance. He'd taken a cab to my flat as soon as he noticed my strange voiceless response to his late call. Sometimes I think my ghost must have been making phonecalls to its well-wishers to save me. When I came to all I wanted was to sleep but since my sleep was full of restless snakes I wanted just not to be. A doctor at the hospital kept talking to me in Punjabi which I don't really understand. They'd called her in to be kind because I was Asian. I wouldn't reply, I played dumb. When he saw me my father said: How could you do this to me? And my usually quiet little sister who'd given birth to twin boys just a month ago shouted: Leave him alone, just leave him alone, can't you see he needs to rest? B was in London at the time and Joan must have said something to her so she turned up too and sat with me for a while before she took her plane to Rome. My abortion of a death, my travesty of a deathbed were turning into a fucking sideshow. Apparently B told someone a few hours later: If he can't get his act together, what can we do for him? And this from Mother Tiger, so compassionate, so tolerant, such a stoic. Sometimes since I've wondered whether it was me she was complaining about or the straight line my life was being diverted to which somehow just didn't permit my dips and breaks, my curves and pauses. Anyway, it had got to her.

The shrink I had to see since it's mandatory to see someone when you damage yourself even if you don't want to asked me what I thought I had that might see me through the next few days, because I said I didn't know where to go when I left his consulting room. (*The world is too big and too small for me. The roads are full of spitting snakes. My intimates are strangers.*) All I have, I said to him, is raw courage and I'm running out of that. You'd better use it then, he said, or what you have left of it. I went home and wrote for hours, the story of my life, dipping and soaring and following no straight line or laiddown track. What emerged was a record of my first fifteen years, my Asian years, seen from the viewpoint of my present. So the two trips 'back' had done their work. I showed it to Joan a few days later. It wasn't really meant to be read, I'd just decided to remember, but I thought I owed him some kind of explanation. I'd deserted poetry for straightforward prose. I didn't know how one went about publishing stories. But I'd sowed the seeds of the mirror-tree, the novella which would become the title story of the collection I published nine years later.

The next year, at thirty, I wrote my first serious story. My behaviourist and I had parted before I grew to depend on him. Joan, disaffected by London's indifference to strangers, had gone via Madrid to Nicaragua. I'd given up singing for good, abandoned Jung and (temporarily) adopted Lacan and Klein. Soon I also learnt to walk beyond the boundaries of my own body to write fictions about others – fables that sent me soaring to the peaks of imagination, stories about rogues and refugees, tales of the woes of love and war. I touched on taboos but chose and choose to write of what I know and from all of myself. I worked, as I do now, with and beyond, not against, my past.

But I still needed the goad of immediate pain to make me write, and planning my life quite carefully to acquire knowledge and avoid conflict meant I wrote seldom and little. It wasn't only pain that made me write, though; also an echoing hollow around me that insisted on being filled up with sound, sound, sound. And the world outside, then, was so scary anyway that writing, usually the source of fear, didn't frighten me.

I stumbled into publishing my work almost unintentionally when I was thirty-two. Some of the time I wrote with my soul in China: not dreaming of a new world order, but rebelling against the dictators sitting inside my skull. I was good with books and words and other writers. A handful of literary editors began to recognize me as a reviewer and critic. The steps to publishing my fiction were steep, but at thirty-five, when I made my first trip to East Asia to do some readings there, I had a good handful of stories in print, and others in various stages of completion. There was a question in the eyes of my peers: When are you publishing a book? I didn't have an answer. Completing something like that could mean admitting I was a writer. I hid behind a critic's jaundiced glasses and then later I took a part-time job as a language teacher at my old college. (When people ask me what I do I still say: I'm a teacher. It's what I went to university for, trained myself to be. I feel more responsible that way. I can't think of writing stories as a job. That's like lovemaking, difficult and a challenge each time and often anticlimactic. I'm baffled when friends tell me they 'work' every day on a fiction.)

B, who loved books, and I had repaired the broken train that commuted between London and Italy, carrying us to each other. The Christmas before I started wanting to write stories again I'd fallen ill with jaundice and B was there. She sat beside my feverish bed almost all day on New Year's Eve and we talked and talked. When I started to be published, she was proud that I'd made something of myself. She thought that if an artist took care of his craft life would take care of him in time. Now the world could see that my white nights and my dun days had a reason. (You're a man dedicated to his craft and ready to struggle for its sake. Life's hard for an idealist. And you aren't aggressive or driven to succeed. That's what they said, she and some others.) But sometimes I'd grow tired of fighting and the old fears returned for a while. Stability is so closely tied to finances: under-worked or overworked, you rarely get the balance right. I kept wondering whether my miniaturist's talent wasn't just too small to survive on walls full of epic murals, whether my voice was too soft to send echoes in halls where boomers bellowed. I was going to spend all my life hiding in libraries, digging up dead sacred monsters, doing literary hackwork, teaching recalcitrant students the intricacies of a foreign tongue. And struggling to earn a makeshift living. Much of the time I was living a temporary life.

As the old decade died, I got a call from a friend in New York telling me B was having an emergency operation for a cancer that had spread from one of her lungs. I'd seen her in the summer, just a few months before. Her father had died in his eighties after a long illness. A few months of silence from her had gone by after that without my worrying too much because I was caught up in the difficult 'mestiere di vivere' as she called it, the business of living, and I knew how much she travelled. She was also working hard at her new Italian career as a photographer. The news of the operation stunned me. I rang the next day. The operation seemed to have been successful. Emerging from anaesthesia, B insisted on taking the phone from her husband's hand and in a drugged voice she said: *Ti voglio tanto bene.* Later she said she didn't remember anything though that made me feel that she really must have meant what she said in her delirium.

I saw her again in the autumn of '90. We'd never been apart for so long in the twelve years we'd known each other. She was staying at a little house in Chelsea. She was so thin she looked transparent and her thick red hair was a grey stubble close to her skull. She was a thousand years old and ageless and more beautiful than ever, as if she'd stepped down from a flying chariot from another planet. I was afraid to hold her as I would have done the year before because I thought I might damage her. I spent the next three or four days with her. Her energy was unabated but I knew it was overdrive because she'd suddenly get exhausted. Chinese Liang, who had become my close friend, said when he saw my pallor: But you, the writer! You should write about it, it'll help. I wanted to push him away but I didn't even say 'never' because he had his own problems, he'd only left the mainland the year before a few weeks after a traumatic divorce and the events at Tiananmen. (Sometimes he'd say: Life's all over, it's all useless, it all comes to nothing. Write a story about me, he said. I did.) I told B he'd said I should write about her. She smiled: One day you might.

The second or third night I'd seen her I started to pray for her because I did pray sometimes though I wasn't conventionally religious. Not to gain anything or bribe God but for silence and tranquillity and the rich poetry of the Arabic words. Compassionate, merciful, benevolent. But this time I was praying for her, begging the source of life not to let her go because I couldn't bear the thought of losing her. After all that I'd lost in my life this one thing would be just too much to bear. She'd given me the unconditional love that no one had ever had for me, nobody had been able to give me. And she wanted so much to go on living. She hadn't yet done enough. As I recited my litany of nine of the ninety-nine beautiful names in cycles of three the string of my rosary broke in my hand and the amber beads scattered, I'd probably squeezed them too hard, and I knew life was rejecting my prayers for her.

I broke down in front of my friend Mona one afternoon though I'm not prone to public tears or outbursts. You shouldn't do this to yourself, it's self torture and it's destructive to you and those around you, Mona was saying. You're becoming a ghost. Let her go. You have to let go of her. Mona knew a lot about pain and a little about death because a bad accident and a botched up operation had left her semi-paralysed before the age of thirty. She'd become addicted to injecting herself with pain killers and opiates which she'd then supplement with large quantities of vodka and wine. For two or three months after that I'd go on occasional wild, savage drinking bouts with her because there was something in me that was bad and needed to be destroyed and I kept feeling that somehow B's illness was a punishment for something I'd done wrong. Then I'd tell Mona she should stop her drinking. She and those bouts with the bottle took me closer to the abyss than I'd ever been before because when I'd suffered from panic attacks and night sweats and a banging heart like a pigeon trapped in a cupboard they'd been spontaneous but this was something else, self-inflicted, a slow suicide. And some Asiatic gene or my puritanical upbringing makes my body reject excessive drinking which is why I'd probably favoured sanctioned chemical substances in the first place but I'd sworn I'd never take those again. I was stick thin and losing more hair. Once more I took a blade in my hand one day and carved patterns on my wrist but this time it was just bravado, a way of showing Mona how much pain I could bear and to beg her not to kill herself with secret drinking. I loved her for a while in my own way but it was the hidden side of me that loved her. I showed it by offering her some kind of tentative love, as if by making her feel like a loved woman I could wipe out my own agony. And for a moment at a time I did but it didn't work, we never went far enough though we'd gone too far and she didn't believe me. She did believe in my writing, though, it was what had drawn her to me in the first place, it was her phantom lover and her rival and her enemy. I wrote about three or four stories that winter when she let go of me, right out of that pain of living, hers and mine, but then a story or two took me beyond our world. The travesty of the Gulf War invaded our heads and for a while everything I wrote was full of that.

I suppose Mona wanted me to split myself in half, leave one part of me with her and take the other off to write. But I couldn't do it. So I ran away, hid in my work. The part-time teaching became almost a full-time occupation. So did the commissions from a respectable literary journal. And my stories started to be noticed. I developed a public persona and split myself not in two but in atoms. One for the literary seminars and soirées where I had to present soundbites. (*I'm always told I write about loss and exile but really I write about bad marriages. I don't feel like an exile, just a nomad. I'm comfortably homeless in six countries and about as many languages.*) One face for my students, one for intimates. And a peaceful facelessness for the books I obsessively read in private. I'd been travelling a bit and had never given up a fantasy of taking myself off, travelling light and settling in some Asian country, perhaps Indonesia. Exile was fashionable and helped the response to my stories though I only claimed chronic expatriate's nostalgia. (I'd never solved the problems of my relationship with England. I still haven't. But Pakistan was hardly in a state to welcome me back.) Atomization needs discipline, though. One of the casualties of living a productive life was Mona, as soon as she saw me come out of the depths she let me let her throw me out which was a relief because my faith in her was dead though in the swill of hate that churned in me there was still some sediment of a kind of loving.

Telling Benedetta about her I shuddered and she said: You shouldn't ever do that. She told me a West African parable by a Sufi sage, about the body or the heart being a fortress with windows full of birds, imprisoned ravens and free-flying doves I think she said. If you send out the good ones they return to their open windows with blessings, but the ravens of rancour and regret, those are bad, they come back and hammer and claw at shuttered windows, they make holes in your bricks and your mortar, they shatter your glass. You shouldn't let the ravens out.

A year and a half later B was dead and I couldn't keep the ravens in. I'd prayed with her at San Francesco's tomb in Assisi the winter after she told me the story. Then the next summer we'd gone to the temples of Java and I think it was at Borobudur that she insisted on going right up to the top and I was behind her in case she tumbled backward. And then she turned round and said goodbye and though I didn't want to hear and no one believed me later I swear I heard her. I came back to London, finished the long story she'd read in Ubud, gave it and its title to a manuscript my friend Hanan was compiling of my stories to pass on to her publisher. I spoke to Benedetta on New Year's Day. Her voice was dim with pain. She'd always dreaded chemotherapy, not the sessions but their terrible after-effects, and I can't remember if she'd had to go through that again. She was disappointed in me because I was screwing up yet another relationship and she wanted to see me settle down. I'd started to walk around in the middle of the night in search of things – including my passport – I'd lost during the day. My capacity to bear relationships, face intimacy, was eroding.

In April, a week before my thirty-eighth birthday, finally goaded by a rejection to do something about a collection of my stories, I took a friend's advice and took my manuscript to her publisher who'd solicited it. A week after my birthday a mutual friend phoned to tell me Benedetta had died that afternoon. When I spoke to those around her they said she'd gone like a warrior. We mustn't mourn. My manuscript was accepted in May. I rewrote and added one more story which I'd recovered from a drawer. The months till November when my book came out flew by. Grief isn't dramatic, it's quiet, a claw that twists in your gut but you can grimace in a way that can make people think you're smiling. But my soul had lost an arm and had to learn to live with only one now – the left, and I'm nominally right handed. It takes time. All the narratives of mourning I'd ever written were preparations for Benedetta's death, but they'd prepared me for nothing. Even the Sufi mystics with their verses about separation as the road to salvation didn't make sense any more. I never wept for Benedetta. (Bathos: a shoddy narrative convention.) But my guilt was stifling me. Why did she never call me? I'd guessed on my birthday that something was wrong but hadn't called, hoping she was alright. And apparently she had been. (*So why didn't you call? Were you angry with me? Why didn't I reach out to you?*) The only time I allowed myself to break was two years later when I admitted that I thought she'd left me in anger.

I dedicated my volume of stories to her. Made the requisite and often irrelevant promotional appearances the protocol of publishing seems to demand. (*What exactly are you selling? Are you a performance poet? Do you write directly in English?*) Then, left voiceless by a chest infection, escaped to the winter sun, my sister in Bangladesh, my cousin in India.

A respite: photographs of my trip show me tranquil and laughing with my arms around my niece and nephews in a canoe on a green stream in the green countryside of Sonargaon. But in India, the tense atmosphere a year after the destruction of the Babri mosque got me down. Another long goodbye, to my mother's country. Fahmida, a Pakistani poet I'd met in London that summer, rang me up in Dhaka, asking me to visit her in Pakistan. We'd talked a lot about roots and affinities, branches and multiple identities. But in the end when I'd bought my ticket I couldn't find her and I didn't make that much delayed trip back to my source, to strife-struck Karachi. I started wondering if I had a source at all. When I came back I was knotted up with pain in my back and legs. I'd eaten carelessly and put on a stone since Benedetta died. Once again, after all those years, I was on medication: treatment for arthritis, almost hallucinatory painkillers. Finally my indefatigable body was giving way: another depleted resource. I lost one of my teaching jobs. A relief. I had to plant roots inside myself now and wait for new shoots, new fruit. So I returned to writing fiction that May – after another birthday, the last of my thirties – to escape from the haplessness that physical pain causes. I had made new friends through my stories and old acquaintances were calling in their debts. I was being asked to write about exile. (And when's the novel due? friends say. You can't making a living out of selling stories. You have to do another book. A novel. I reply: I like short fictions. I dry up after forty pages. I like Pramoedya but I don't want to be him.) But I wrote.

I turned forty. Middle age came easily. I'd come to the age of reason, probably not lost my right arm, just left it numb and learned to use the left. I might yet learn to be ambidextrous. But then the fears returned: another failed relationship, underemployment, the aridity of research and critical writing, the inability to tell stories, the sense of time flowing away and leaving me stranded on an island of unfulfilled fantasies. I was silent. The ravens I'd let fly had come back to roost; they were banging at my walls and shuttered windows.

One night in April I saw a documentary about writers on Prozac. I was tempted and told my doctor. To her horror. But instead I wrote a story, about Benedetta and Bali. The restless ravens drove me on. All truths turned into fictions, identities disguised, pain transformed into poetry. Maybe, in the end, writing's my Prozac.

I wrote through October. I could see the end of a new collection. I'd talk to my friend Eun about Sopyonje, a magnificent film we'd both seen, full of the music of separation and unfulfilled yearning. Then in the autumn rain we talked about poetry and art and catharsis and she said: Koreans see suffering as a sequence of knots to be untied, a process that goes on and on. You can see it in our dances: a series of movements of unknotting. The dance of life, I said to her later. And I knew that even if my grief were ever to subside, it would take me years to learn those gestures, I hadn't learnt the steps to the dance of unknotting. And if I did I'd be bereft because sometimes the knots are all I have left of Benedetta. And late that Friday night I began this story. I don't think I'll ever write about those years again.

And I've left out so much in this bare chronicle: the colons and clauses and commas I relish, the punctuation of irony and detachment, the syntax that transforms private anguish into signs and wonders. I've left out the gift of laughter, the ability to mock myself and turn my trials into tales, the bubbles that float up when least expected to subvert the pompous, the earnest and the pedantic. I've left out the journey from the shallows of erotic tension to the depths of friendship, and the pleasures of friendship which make my day: listening to Liu's tales of falling in love again, walking in the wet November leaves exchanging stories with Hanan, welcoming Mai back from Beirut, hearing Mimi read out her beautiful poems to the music of the santur in spring or her winter voice on my machine a few hours ago telling me she's missed me, talking about the Silla lyrics of So Chongju over hot rice and steaming sesame-flavoured noodles on a cold December night with Eun. I've left out all my joys and loves, which I need a lifetime and the distance of fiction to recount, and the embers and ashes of forbidden tears: those are hidden in the pauses of my fiction.

But in writing about Benedetta I've written about learning the language of absolute love, my first language, about losing and wondering if anything is gained from what is lost, written with the hand I thought was frozen, the arm that hung, useless, by my side. After these movements of unknotting it still aches. But perhaps, for a moment, my hands and the birds are peaceful, the white birds and the black, the ravens, the doves. Loneliness joins hands with itself. Somewhere Benedetta, Amata. And then the night.

The Actress's Tale

Helena had a nervous breakdown from drinking too much because her husband the director didn't like her work. She spent two weeks in an expensive nuthouse. When she'd been without work for months she accepted a role in an East End theatre. Forty-five seats above a pub. She played an aging actress who fell in love with a gambler and had to sing a torch song. The gambler was played by a guy shorter than her and eight years younger who had a shaved head and wore three studs and a ring in his left ear. He was from Hiroshima and sang opera. He reeked of garlic and peed on street corners but she took him home and he kissed her for a while but then he fell asleep in her bed and snored after saying he couldn't share one so she made up a bed on the sofa and he made very soft love to her with his tongue and fingers at six in the morning with the birds screeching before going to sleep again and then getting up to take a shower and setting off for his singing lesson. That night he acted as if nothing had happened but a few nights later he followed her home and offered to cook from his bag of provisions which were pasta and butter and a lot of garlic. She'd expected raw fish. She laid a table in her backgarden. A big red paperlantern moon hung over their heads. There were gnats. He ate like a waste disposal machine and drank six beers and peed in her frogpond. Then he breathed garlic on her and drooled on her face and slept and snored and woke up and made clumsy dawn love and slept again and showered and went to his singing lesson. Another night he

took her to his fourteenth-floor studio near Canary Wharf with a view
of the river and the boats and he played Javanese music all night long
and then at first light he called her a cab on his mobile because he said
he only had one narrow bed to sleep on and couldn't bear to share. It
cost her fifteen pounds she didn't have to get home and she had to get
out on Charing Cross Road for some money from a machine that
wouldn't work but the cabby recognized her and gave her a free ride.
On the last night of the show the man from Hiroshima got drunk at
the party and called her a mad old bag because he guessed she'd been
angry and he said it's the Buddha's birthday and I've been to the
temple and decided to conserve my yang energies for my art. She
hadn't been sure how to get rid of him. She'd taken him out to dinner
one night and said goodnight at her doorstep in South Hampstead.
He'd taken the night bus back to Mile End.

ꙮ

She went to the Air India office and booked a holiday she'd read about
in a free magazine she'd found in the hall of her red brick apartment
block. She'd grown up in Malaya but all she could remember of Asia
was slimy lizards and snakes. She flew from Delhi to the Taj Mahal and
then to Khajuraho. She was booked into a fancy hotel she was sure was
haunted because the walls echoed with comings and goings and
whisperings all night. She'd taken a bit to drinking again but only
Indian beer because it was hot and no one told her you don't come to
India in summer. She saw the erotic friezes and found them pretty but
disturbing because she couldn't see love in the blank eyes of the lovers.
She found a café opposite the ruins where she met a man with a
moustache who looked at her kindly and introduced her to a couple
of French midwives who were here to get married. They looked about
twenty-four. He invited her to dinner that night at a villa he said he
had in the jungle in Panna nearby. He'd be there in his jeep to pick her
up at eight, he said. When she looked at the card he'd given her she
saw he was Prince Ranjit Singh of Ranchipur.

She'd been away two weeks but she knew it was nearly time to go back so she phoned her agent after two stiff doses of Indian gin spiked with fresh lime juice. She couldn't believe what he told her. She had two offers, one for a sitcom and the other to play Phaedra at the National. Then she had another big gin and got dressed for the dinner and when she looked at herself in the mirror she saw her sleek black hair and her skin smooth and brown and thought that at forty-nine she looked good again. The two midwives were in the jeep. The boy's name was Marc and the girl was Corinne. They came from somewhere in Northern Brittany. They were going to have a Hindu wedding here with an elephant and a brass band. She was small and blonde with green eyes and he was medium height and dark but his eyes were silver. The party was up a tree where the prince had built a house that tourists could stay in with a little loo and everything. They sat on a wooden terrace perched on the lower branches of the tree. Helena suffered from vertigo. The prince served a clear dry liquid from a kerosene bottle. It looked like water and tasted like fire but sweet. The prince said: There's a legend here about a girl called Mahua whose stepmother was cruel to her and she turned into a white flower. This drink is made of cloves, cardamoms and that flower. The drink and the flower are also called Mahua. You can drink as much as you like and you won't have a hangover tomorrow. She drank. Fireflies flew up towards the rising red moon. Hibiscus flashed red here and there. She remembered walking barefoot that morning with her sandals in her hand across cool sharp stones in a stream with the morning sun overhead. They ate hot snacks with their drinks. Then Marc sang *A la claire fontaine* on his guitar. Later the prince whispered to Corinne who asked her to sing and she did. This is what I've been called here for, to sing for my supper, but it doesn't matter. Me in the world's most beautiful place. Bewitched, bothered and bewildered am I. I've left behind that city where the slimy drops running down drainpipes remind you that happiness is a dirty word. She could feel the prince's knee pressing against hers though his thin brittle wife was there too drinking whisky not Mahua. Marc was pouring more and more

Mahua into her glass and Marc was staring at her and his silver eyes made her head spin worse than the silver liquid stream of Mahua in her. She wanted to make love to him with an anguish that was coming from her ribs and had little to do with her thighs. There was a ladder leading to the the highest branches and Marc, shouting, was standing beneath it. She was conscious of her bladder and got up to pee. Marc stretched out a hand and took hers and said: Come on up with me. But I suffer from vertigo, she said. Come on, I'm holding on to you, you won't fall down, he said and she moved to climb the ladder behind him. Corinne was standing up now. Suddenly Helena saw a lizard in the branches and screamed. Marc was pulling her up the ladder. Leave her alone, you drunk, can't you see she's afraid, she'll fall, Corinne shouted in French. Helena felt sick now and dizzy. Corinne was looking at her with a look like the man from Hiroshima's that said: you silly old slag, don't you know you're ridiculous.

— Can you drop me back to the hotel, Helena said to the prince after a polite intermission.

At the hotel the next morning she saw them again but they ignored her till Marc took Corinne's hand and brought her over to Helena's table. Corinne's eyes and face were puffy and they'd obviously been fighting. The waiter brought tea but Helena never took milk in hers. Marc hadn't said a word but now he got up and walked away.

— It was a great night and you sang so beautifully, Corinne said.

— I have a hangover though the prince said I wouldn't, Helena said.

— O that Marc. He gave you too much to drink. He always does that. I'm sorry.

Just then Marc walked up with a plate of fresh sliced limes.

— For your tea, he said. I know you hate milk.

At Khajuraho airport, she felt sorry she hadn't slept with the prince who'd obviously wanted to, because it would have been nice to take an Indian to bed in India. The gin last evening had made her cloudy but she was sure she'd heard her agent right, her husband wanted to direct her as Phaedra at the National. She wasn't going to do it because it would be fun to say No to him and she didn't want to play another greedy tragic old bat. And Malcolm Masterson, whom she'd nearly slept with once when she was twenty and he was thirty and they'd played in Rep together, was playing her neighbour in the sitcom. He'd been widowed recently. This was his comeback appearance. It would be good to perform with him again.

The Lost Cantos of the Silken Tiger

Potiphar's Court

A stranger came to a strange new city, the most famous in a country that was only five years old. His name was Yusuf; they called him the silken tiger, for the verses he wrote were as smooth as silk, but had the soft-footed ferocity of a tiger's leap. Welcomed in every salon of the town, he purposefully made his way, however, to the court of the great and celebrated Minister of Culture, who was known as Potiphar for the powers and privileges he enjoyed. His real name was forgotten; but not so that of his wife, the beautiful Zuleikha, who was as famous for the beauty of her green eyes and golden hair as she was for the exquisite poems and songs she wrote.

This is how Yusuf arrived at Potiphar's court. Listen:

When Potiphar's wife heard that this bard and minstrel of the old country had crossed the border to find a home in the new land, she demanded that he appear in the court to engage with her in a battle of words. For she was well-known in the town as an incomparable poet among women; but none among the versifying men of the town had dared to pit his wit against hers, laughing behind their embroidered sleeves at the ignominy and folly of competition with a woman. In her presence, they only affected to praise the skill of her metre and the charm of her delicate images; but Zuleikha was too clever a woman to believe that their flattery was sincere. Behind the veil of their compliments she discerned another veil, of mendacity; and behind that, too, a gossamer layer of jealousy and envy and fear.

As for the silken tiger, his reputation for romance and fearlessness had preceded him; he lived as he wrote and he wrote as he lived. Zuleikha, at the ripening age of forty-three, longed for a true and vital rival. Not for her the sarcastic asides or the simpering similes of the city's court poets; nor the butterfly spin or homespun homilies of the court poetesses who, afraid to challenge their peers among men, stayed delicately confined in the verbal and visual decorum of inner courtyards.

So Zuleikha summoned Yusuf to the outer courtyard of Potiphar's home. In those first years after ridding themselves of the empire's yoke, the city's intellectuals were rediscovering, with fervour, their own heritage, and peasant craftsmanship, too; the white chambers of Potiphar's house were carpeted in straw matting and sparsely furnished, with mirror-worked cushions, some stools of straw and wood, a few patchwork seats, a single divan. Zuleikha was dressed in a stark ensemble of black brushed with gold, cut daringly low on shoulder and bosom; its textures enhanced, with unerring brilliance, her brilliant colouring. Yusuf, dressed in white, his collar open at the neck, looked, with his unruly bright hair, as if he had just come in from the cricket-field. The stranger-poet, thirteen years younger than Zuleikha, was also her rival in beauty; or, to tell the truth, her twin, for he like her was small and slight and seemed to be made of bronze and jade, and framed in spun gold. His hair, however, unlike Zuleikha's unaided by artifice, was the colour of flame, and his narrow eyes showed traces of Tatar blood. Zuleikha saw Yusuf as she saw her own reflection in glass, but while her mirrored image bored her for she had no true rival, the impact of her beauty stunned her when revealed to her in another's features and form.

Yusuf began the recital with a series of quatrains in traditional mode; Zuleikha responded with an elaborately asymmetrical composition in free verse, which had only recently become the mode among the literati, and was still disdained by many among the old guard. Yusuf dramatically raised a slender hand to his brow, and after a moment's pondering, improvised, in an identical rhythm, a verse permeated with gentle humour:

Like Sabah, you mistake a mirror for a lake:
You need a Sulaiman to show you the truth
of love.

Zuleikha responded with a few stammered and incoherent words, followed by a deafening silence. She was enraged, but her aesthetic discernment was pressing upon her to concede the victor's prize, when Yusuf heroically announced: 'Yours is the original; mine a mere imitation. To you, the victory of the beautiful word. '

To Zuleikha, her victory tasted of defeat: she had not wrested it with her own artful strategies from the hands of the vanquished; it had been too willingly conceded. Her chagrin was aided all the more by the couplet that, before Yusuf's tribute to her, had welled up within her and frozen on her lips:

You, like Yusuf, turn your back upon my hapless love
A proud Zuleikha I, who, love-crazed, bleed when you appear.

But as these words – these naked, shaming words – began to play upon the redness of her lips and she, in her shame, was struggling to stop them from escaping the cage of her thoughts, Zuleikha became aware of another burst of shaming red: the waterfall that, unbidden, had begun to flow, for the first time in three or four years, between her thighs. For like our mother Eve, who as a punishment for the sin of plucking the forbidden grains from the ear of wheat had known the pain of menstruation, the gaining of unlawful knowledge had caused Zuleikha, too, to bleed.

She determined to win and then break Yusuf's heart. But Yusuf's heart was there for the taking and the breaking: no challenge at all to the proud poet. And a tender companionship had grown between the young man and the powerful Potiphar; they would spend all their time together, comparing the verses of poets dead and living, for Potiphar, too, was a learned man. We would not be rash to assume that the silken tiger had crept into his master's chamber to leap and kill; but it was not the blood of Potiphar's heart that would slake his ardent thirst, only the melting of the icy orb of concealed desire in Zuleikha's beautiful bosom. One quiet afternoon, the poet wept and declared his burning passion, and the lonely Zuleikha opened to him the portals of her heart.

Zuleikha lay in her lover's arms, sipping pale sparkling wine from fluted crystal, gold-tipped Sobranie between jade-painted finger tips in the splendour of her French boudoir (for Zuleikha, the daughter of a Turcophile Prince and his exotic Turkish mistress, had early acquired a taste for things imported and European, which was indulged in the sanctity of the inner chamber where for many years she had slept alone, since her husband had long since expressed his preference for plump and very young pigeons of both sexes). She listened to Yusuf's songs and sang him her verses, encouraged to be with him by her doting but negligent husband who (like Arthur in Camelot) wanted her amused while he occupied himself with state affairs. This ballad of desire and satiation was sung by the city's courtesans and minstrels, reaching on the airwaves the ears of other cities. And while the scroll of love unfolded, trouble was brewing in the country. The benign rulers of the land of the pure and the just had seen to it that the stalwarts of the honest bourgeoisie were permanently safe and protected, and that only such poverty persisted as allowed the less needy to perform their duties of almsgiving – for a structured society means a stable land. But the military had taken power, surreptitiously, and days, like prayer beads, were counted by the faithful who feared a *coup d'état* and a subsequent takeover by the country's most powerful young general, a man whose regimental mind and puritanical spirit fascinated the mighty Potiphar, who believed – as he held that art and religion should be kept apart from state affairs – that might, right and order were synonyms, triple faces of one, omnipotent creator.

Zuleikha, ever more keenly, listened, at the wrought-iron table in the glass-enclosed patio that served as their parlour, to her husband's confidences, imparted over crisp triangles of toast and marmalade (or home-farmed honey from her husband's country properties, her token concession to Potiphar's nationalist inclinations in this room which was, like her boudoir, furnished according to her pleasure.) Potiphar's considerable verbal energies were at their most potent at this early hour; in the first years after their marriage, husband and wife had spoken of music and miniatures and verse, but now the duties of his calling burdened Potiphar with lethal secrets, which he shared with his wife – as silence is a sad state for a prolix man of high and fixed opinions.

'The General – let us not mention his name even *devant les domestiques* – is poised to coerce old Firaon into signing his resignation,' Potiphar told Zuleikha. 'He will then persuade us to persuade him to establish martial rule to counteract disorder and chaos, for Firaon is still a much-loved man. After a decent interval, when army rule is dissolved, he will take the ruler's chair as the undisputed leader of our land. '

'And does this make you happy?' Zuleikha asked, her alabaster brow furrowing, her green eyes narrow with concern.

'No – I think, for the moment, that we should let things ride; later, when the old man's ready to go, we can bring the General in with at least some semblance of democratic behaviour. But the General and the army are afraid of elections. What fools they are. Don't they know that no one – I repeat, no one – is prepared to offer their services to a position of absolute power? We all prefer to rule behind the scenes; we counteract the military's absolute influence by influencing the military. '

. . . Sated with loving, lips swollen like plums and green eyes shadowed with circles of tired green, tigerish limbs entwined with the limbs of her young tamed tiger in her purple-sheeted bed, Zuleikha told Yusuf, three hours after her conference with Potiphar, of her husband's apprehensions. For she, a brave and brilliant woman held back by her sex in this land of patriarchs, trusted the finely-tuned judgement of the stranger-poet, who was an idealist and a pacifist. He would allay her fears. Or so she thought.

The rest of this prose version of the story – if it ever existed – is lost. The above chapter was published in Mah-e-Kamil, the journal of the Circle of Luminaries, in the month of the cataclysmic events of which we are about to learn. But let us not race ahead of our tale. So. Listen:

The Poet of the Many-coloured Coat

Forty-three years later, a man, living in London, a cold city of the North, was struggling to complete the manuscript of a book about a group of poets in the then fair and self-regarding seaside city of Karachi, who styled themselves The Circle of Luminaries. Their aim was to dedicate their lives to art and only to art; their poems, novels and stories would eschew political comment; the journal of their glittering circle was called *The Full Moon*; they disdained the didactic pontifications of a rival group, The Association of Progressive Writers, who believed in art for the sake of food, bread and a house for all, and admired Stalin and the Soviet Union. The Luminary-in-Chief was Agha Abdul Aziz, who wrote under the pseudonym of Abbas Zulfiqar, and even today holds a position of great respect in the annals of our literature. He is credited with having introduced Woolf, Joyce and Kafka to our prose writers, and Eliot, Pound and Rimbaud to our tradition-haunted poets. The man who aimed to be the chronicler of the Luminaries, our diligent researcher and would-be social historian – his name is Mehran Malik, and we can assume he is the chamber which contains the echoes of the many voices of this tale – discovered, during his researches, a strange, compelling fact, which created a hiatus, a missing chapter, in his book.

This is how it happened. Listen:

A revolutionary poet of renown – who, exiled from our country for his unproved part in a famous early conspiracy, had for many years taught cultural history, from a neo-Marxist standpoint, in the west's leading academies – was persuaded to give a seminar on his verse, which he swore he had long since abandoned (with a brief, biting volume of poems in English, dissecting with bitterness his abandonment of the Soviet dream and his ideological Marxism). The seminar was part of a conference on Indic Literatures at the Academy of Oriental Studies in Bloomsbury. The occasion that had persuaded him to appear in an assembly of *litterateurs* was the publication of a slim volume he had authored, a memoir of mordant beauty tellingly entitled *Nights in Hell*, which told of incarceration in Pakistan, release, exile, painful years of ostracism and penury in India, and eventual departure for the West. It was also a return – albeit in prose – to his long-forsaken mother tongue.

Our illustrious poet appeared in a suit of elegant cut and flamboyant fabric – grey silk, with crimson thread woven in imperceptible subtlety into the sombre texture. He was now an enlightened scholar of Islamic dissension, as famous for his philosophical diatribes against Said, Rushdie and Aijaz Ahmad as he was for his unconventional take on Islam. To hear him read was a great pleasure, for his poems, in our best twentieth-century tradition, took on political issues with grace, dignity, compassion and painful honesty. He had, however, requested that no questions be asked about his hurried and notorious departure from Pakistan – was it exile, or defection? He would also refuse to reply to queries about his part in the great communist conspiracy to assassinate the prime minister of the time and the leading General, in 1953.

He read with throwaway elegance, raising, from time to time, a slender manicured hand to his hair, which still bore the traces of its erstwhile flaming colour.

Then a request came, from the audience, for a love poem. The speaker who voiced it was a translator and budding feminist historian of our literature, Rubina 'Neeli' Raja, who insists on the quotation marks around her middle name, as a sign, she says, of the dialectic between the Self in its constant process of creation, and Family History. (She was in the habit of saying Herstory, until Mehran, who was both a rival and a sometime fellow-traveller, pointed out that in the Latin origin of the word there was no gendered pronoun implicated, and in most romance languages 'history' was indistinguishable from 'story'. Now, since her discovery of Cixous and her own work-in-progress on Aarzou, the Luminaries' leading feminine constellation who was, according to La Raja, a great writer negated by the critics only for her vast reputation as a paradoxical populist story-teller, La Raja speaks of my-story-pronounced-mystery; or Wombanview.)

But we wander from our story. So. Listen carefully:

When Yusuf Reza – for that is the name of our revolutionary poet and radical scholar – had finished reciting his tender and slightly lascivious love-poem, La Raja, dressed in turquoise sackcloth and polka-dotted flat crepe, her fine hair gathered behind her head into a variegated snood, stood up in the audience and declaimed: 'Is it true that this poem was dedicated to a character conspicuous in her absence from your book: Aarzou Baig?'

The septuagenarian poet flushed to his flaming roots.

'And to her husband, Agha,' he responded. 'And both of them are mentioned, in passing, in my very subjective and impressionistic memoir, which is exactly that and clearly not a sociohistorical document.'

'But your political views were of a different colour from the Circle of Luminaries – what was your connection with Agha and Aarzou?'

'There are, in art, no sectarian banners or political colours. That is why I left the Progressive Writers and refused to be part of any coterie. I abandoned poetry because my ideals told me the beliefs of my time and my commitment to art as a tool of protest were equally false . . . I recognized my failure to reconcile my goals. And only now, at this great old age, I can see, from my distance, the relative merits of my work, the intensity of my passion for medium and message alike, the articulation of my commitment to a common humanity, the only statement worth anything.'

'Have you read Aarzou's sequence of poems, "The Silken Tiger Cantos?"' La Raja persisted, to the chagrin of the session's chairman. 'Could you comment on her version of historically documented events? What gaps do you think it fills in for the layperson? And, finally, how do you feel about her portrayal of you? For you are undoubtedly the silken tiger of the title. She hasn't even bothered to change your name. '

'Let our learned friend speak,' said the venerable Yusuf Reza to the irate and embarrassed chairman. 'Aarzou's is one version of history, her own version. I must have another: and there are too many unknown factors. History is one part myth and one part mystery; so if we choose to call the other version myth, let's say I prefer to keep my story a mystery. '

The next day – the last but one of his stay in London – Yusuf Reza refused Mehran Malik the interview to which he had earlier consented; he cancelled it when he discovered that the younger writer was working on the lives and infamous times of Messrs Agha and Baig. He was conspicuously absent from La Raja's presentation, entitled 'Myth and the Feminine Mystique – Early Women Writers of Pakistan', which she presented that day. Mehran, deprived of the opportunity to converse with a man who he felt held at least one key to the mystery he sought so ardently to solve, decided to do a spot of sleuthing and see if the discussion would yield some fresh fruits of knowledge. After all, Aarzou, whom we now dismiss as typical of everything we disdain in the writings of romanticizing women, was for a time the Circle of Luminaries' leading luminary. But Malik had thought that it was her laconic grace and her ravishing, deliberately artificial beauty, crowned by her gilded hair and her position as Agha's wife, that made her so.

The Legend of Potiphar's Wife

'Do you remember?' Rubina 'Neeli' Raja said, shuffling her papers on the podium. Listen:

'After a long, long silence – of ten years or more, if you discount the embarrassing nationalist eulogies to which she lent her name during the '65 war – Aarzou produced the most splendid work of her career, the epic poem "The Silken Tiger", a reinterpretation of Jami's Persian *masnavi*, based on the romance of Yusuf and Zuleikha. She had already attempted a prose version of the story, of which one chapter was published as you have already been told by our learned friend Mr Malik, and as most of you will know, only three cantos of the verse version appeared in her life time; the fourth, which I am about to reveal to you today, was not only completed a mere four days before her death, but was not included in *Jaan-e-Aarzou*, the edition of her Complete Works edited, compiled and introduced by her grieving husband. It has so far only appeared in an avant-garde Karachi journal called *today*, and in my translation in America.

'The poem is set in an unnamed land – reminiscent now of Turkey, now of Iraq and now of Southern France, but slowly, slowly unveiling the sea breezes, the burning sun and the outlying desert of her adopted city, Karachi – in a time which, we gradually discover, is her own, for among the Circassian handmaidens, haunted marble halls, ruby-studded lutes and star-spangled chiffon veils there are telephones, airplanes, gramophone records and high-powered political assemblies. Now Aarzou had always set her fictions in a romanticized Orient – and this, I will claim, was her husband's influence upon her or rather his editorial tyranny, because he did not believe in direct commentary or social realism. He was also afraid of offending the English, the militaries, and all men in boots. Aarzou's first novel, written in her own name when she was barely sixteen, is set in the first decade of our century, in a recognizable Hyderabad, the city she really came from. But editions now available, all of them reprints of a second edition, bear the signs of her husband's erasures; cities, names and dates are rabidly discarded. Agha also created the myth of Aarzou's exotic origins, hinting that she, like the heroine of her stories who was always called Tamanna Khanum, was the daughter of a high-ranking officer and his Turkish concubine. According to this legend, Aarzou was born in Istanbul, in a palace by the Bosphorus, and had grown up in Baghdad, where Agha, visiting the Orient's pearls on a literary pilgrimage, glimpsed her through a beaded curtain. That her father was a medium-ranking official in the Nizam of Hyderabad's employ is true, but her mother, to the best of my knowledge, was the daughter of a Sayyad cleric from Lahore. Her marriage to Agha resulted from an exchange of letters and missives, an outpouring of youthful poetry from her and dispatches of critical prose from him. Her caste-conscious parents only consented to this union with the much older *litterateur* because she was nearly twenty, a great age for a woman. She also flew kites, rode a motorbike, smoked black cigarettes and wrote very daring novels.

'Aarzou's later fictions are veiled in haziness – edited and censored, as my research among her manuscripts proves, by her husband, who nevertheless allows her the negative feminist endings which remain her form of radical protest against the stifling bureaucratic class, just one step below the nobility, into which she was born. Now we are all too ready to dismiss the lush romanticism and exotic locales of her work – but careful study will reveal to you that, in spite of Agha's tampering, Aarzou's is a powerful voice of protest, even a pioneering voice. In this great and graceful poem she tackles an even bigger problematic – that of the relation between art and politics in a newly created nation. Her writer husband, she prophetically casts as a bureaucrat – and that, of course, is what he later became, condoning and colluding with, by his deafening silences and his insistence on art for its own sake, the placing of clamps on the mouths of radicals and of women. Aarzou staged herself as Potiphar's wife – an early feminist struggle to present a woman mad, bad and dangerous, for hers is a story of revenge and betrayal.

'This is the last, lost canto of which I spoke. Forgive my clumsy

English rendition of Zuleikha's glorious lyrical diction, which derives its force from its radical combination of modernist form and traditional imagery. Let me read it to you.

Listen to the flute, as it sings its song of separation. '

The Lost Canto of the Silken Tiger

Seabirds stretch their wings,
sheltering them from the
sun's heat. Sky and sea
share a bed, are one.

The lovers ride the foam. Wave
licks hoof: The black
horse falls. The seam of her
man's brocaded jacket is torn.
I will mend it for you myself,
she says. He blanches:
she will not let it go.

Hidden in its pocket's seam, she
finds the itinerary of her lover's
plan to kill the president and
his opponents, the military
leaders who are contemplating
a coup d'etat. So they would
rid their land, in one sharp
move, of its oppressors. He is
in league with a rebel group.
He believes in equality for all,
an end to exploitation by princes
and viziers. For he is a tiger
in disguise as a lamb, a renegade

and rebel, who receives instructions
from the land across the border, and
from another mighty, fire-breathing empire.
The rain clouds swarm.

She cannot believe what seems to be
the truth – that her lover has used
her, without mercy, for his own needs.
Unwittingly she has served as a spy,
given away the country's secrets. She
has been a traitor to her high ideals
and her hopes of peace and prosperity.

Looking in the mirror she sees
the hollows and caverns beneath
the heavy paint on her face. She
is an aging woman looking for love,
deprived of love: only in her poems
has she ever fulfilled her deepest
velvet desires. On the parched desert
sand, the rain falls. It soothes the
sandstorm.

When he comes to her mirrored boudoir,
she faces him with her new knowledge
of his treacheries. They encompass
arson, gun-running, bombing and
the illegal possession of arms.

He tells her that he does love her,
but this love he feels for her,
this consuming desire that enflames
his entrails and his belly, must be
subjugated to a higher good.

For there are torments in life
far greater than the agony of love,
and greater bliss than the fevered
joy of union. Outside, the rain sings
a relentless song. The wind howls.

She asks him to walk with her in
her secret garden. She tells him
she will try to understand, to
follow him, fulfil his dreams.
She will not heed the rain.

He says: You are only a woman, a
mere feeble creature in spite
of your tiger graces. And when my
chore is done, I will leave your
country for two years, to study
in that great, great land where
visions of equality and fraternity
are realized. I will bring back
its grand and gracious messages
to the oppressed of our barren,
rain-starved earth.

And Yusuf tells Zuleikha: If
in those years you read the
holy books of the prophets
of fraternity, you may be
redeemed, and survive in the
new order.

If not, you must go the way of
all oppressors, into the dungeons
where your kind have tortured,

imprisoned and tormented
the wretched of the earth.

But you are a singer and a poet,
she says, you are a man of dreams.
Where are those visions you showed
me of peace and happiness? Of music
and flowers, of miniatures and pastel
tapestries and verses of our restless
longings, painted in gold letters
on screens of white silk?

Peace can only be achieved after
struggle: blood must be spilt
to make a bed for rivers of milk
and honey. So the silken tiger
says. This is the only poem I know,
the only prayer I recite. All I said
before, the words I used to seduce
you, were trifles, gewgaws to bemuse a
vain and lonely woman. You call yourself
a poet? You sell your words, as a harlot
sells her flesh, for flattery.

His words pierce her bones and
the flute of her being. The hot
rain pours upon her, licks her skin
like a flame. The wind howls.

Poetry, she thinks, is the music
of my soul. It is the cool air
I drink, the sun that warms my back
and the soft rain that refreshes me.
It is the snow tenderly melting into blue

waterfalls that flow from the mountains
of this land I love.

Poetry is my being, the god himself
who in his glory, lives within
this altar of my body and my breasts.
Poetry is the blood that flows from
my belly, and runs down my thighs.
And who called forth the blood from me?
Yusuf, my twin, Yusuf, my Adam, my
peacock, my snake, my Satan. Who pierced
my wood like a flute, in the agony of
separation? But I was mistaken. He never
was my reflection, I was his. (I lost
myself, a willing wanderer, in the mirrors
of his love.)

And if the mirror breaks, where
will my love go? And if my blood
ceases to flow, how will I compose
my songs? For the music of my words
is his love. Allah! A string breaks.
My voice dies.

He walks away from her as sunset,
like a wild duck, spreads its
wounded wing. Alone, she wanders
in her ornamental garden. White
geese float on its mirrored pond.
Hibiscus petals fall gently on
her bowed golden head. She crushes
underfoot the bruised bodies of white
blossoms. The cruel scent of frangipani
fills the air.

The wild duck cries: I am forgotten.
A wild boy has wounded my wing with
a stone from his slingshot. My mate
left with the north-bound horde,
and I'm left broken on a burning beach.
The sea boils.

She stays there as the night turns
from stone to water and then to
black glass, reflects the jade pendant
of the moon, surrounded by a thousand
jewelled candles. Now her flaming tears
have turned to anger's ice. The moon
flees. The flute is silent now.

Dressed carefully for the occasion
in unadorned black, with only a single
thick silver bracelet on her wrist – a gift,
bought for her by Potiphar from a peasant's
market, she hitherto disdained – she goes to
her husband: reveals her infidelity,
says she will pay the price of her betrayal.
She unveils each detail of the plan her
faithless man has concocted with his companions.
She begs him to commend the conspirators to
justice and retribution: Despatch them to Hell.
Outside, the drums beat and the rain sighs.
The scent of frangipani fills the air.

Potiphar is grim-faced, silent. He looks away
from her. He cannot meet the candour of her
green eyes. He orders an investigation: The
grave and terrible work of justice and
retribution will, at his command, be done.
Then, Pilate-like, he rinses his hands.

The conspiracy is uncovered, the conspirators
disbanded and disembowelled. But then, how
strange! Potiphar relents. Perhaps the strange
poison of a fledgeling love, a bird fallen
thirsty from its fragile nest, beseeches him.
He pleads for the silken tiger's life.
But before they exile Yusuf from the land,
the masters leave their fatal mark. They
castrate him with red-hot coals, make a
limping travesty of the silken tiger. His
flute is broken now: its voice dies. It
is midsummer and the clouds have burst.
The drums have fallen silent. The wind sings
its ballads and the sweet rain falls.

Zuleikha, like a masked Noh dancer or a
dirge-singer in Muharram, mauls
her face with her long nails. She
tears her hair. She damns herself
for her deed. Allah, you break my
strings and no one hears. The beads
of my prayers are scattered now. I
must calculate the days of separation
on the flanges of my fingers till their
lines rub out. But then, when I meet Yusuf
in heaven, he will turn his face from me.
So let me rot in hell. And if God is
forgiving, paradise a dream, then let me
be without rest, let me sleep
without dreaming.

Her blood cries. She hears its last flow.
It tells her it has ceased forever.

'It is one of the most powerful and moving portrayals of a woman's rage turned inwards in ours or any other literature,' La Raja concluded. 'And it gains its strength because – more than any other work by this fabulist who is also a deeply autobiographical writer – this is a memoir, a testament, a calling to witness, a proud confession of sin – a mistresswork of my-story that uncovers one of our time's greatest mysteries: allegorizes and rewrites the destiny of a nation, how it is subverted by a woman's powerful passion and revenge. '

Yusuf Tells his Stinging Tale

'Methinks the lady doth protest too much, and I'll tell you why', said Yusuf Reza to Mehran Malik, two days later. He had changed his mind about the interview; he had rung Malek at his office and told him it was merely a dental appointment that had caused the cancellation of so pleasurable an encounter. They could now meet, he said, the problem of the plaguing tooth being temporarily resolved. They were sitting in the salon of a dignitary of the Pakistan High Commission, over tea in fragile porcelain, fritters and tiny cucumber sandwiches – for we have forgotten to mention that Yusuf Reza, in these changed and newly democratic times, was now welcome to visit the land of his abandoned dreams whenever he so chose, and this embassy dignitary was his sister's son.

Yusuf ran his hand through his flame-and-grey locks. 'Aarzou Khanum's poem is autobiographical', he said, 'except for one detail. Of course, Aarzou – the Lord rest her fantasizing soul – has exaggerated everything. Poetic license, we could say. I never was as much of a didactic Marxist as she makes out in her poem; certainly never a Communist or as pro-Soviet as those Luminary bastards would continue to write about me in their pretentious pseudo-philosophical treatises on our culture. More of an anarchist, really; I still am. Food and justice for all, but I like my champagne and my cigarillos, and never denied that my old man was a landowner, though once I went with some of my mates to create some mayhem in our own country house, smashed a chandelier, stole some silver, wrecked an amethyst fountain. And as for verse – I don't want to flatter myself, and old Agha's already taken enough credit for moulding Aarzou as the Embodiment of the Feminine in our collective soul, but I saw the potential for true greatness in her as soon as we met. In return, she helped me with my verses, too, told me how to soften the crudeness of my message with the poetry of word and sound: Statements were always clearest when understated. And I also have to say that she had the most beautiful style in the business. You should see the effect it had when she lent it, anonymously, to the speeches the revolutionaries made. I never, never jeered at her verse – only told her she should be less raw and painfully ingenuous in the expression of her pain and her beliefs. Even then I understood too well the hazardous, tightrope walk of polemical art. And you can see from the Yusuf and Zuleikha poems how well she learnt the ploys of her craft. The rhetoric of revolution she attributes to Yusuf has all the bejewelled lavishness – and some of the self-indulgent bombast – of our youthful utterances. But if any one was a true revolutionary, she was. Yes, my boy, we were fellow radicals, co-conspirators. And she was closer to the edge of the precipice than I; she knew about plans and projects that I, who was ten years younger and a relative newcomer to her city, could only guess at.

'She was never the vain pleasure seeker that Zuleikha occasionally appears to be in the poem. No hedonist, certainly; even in moments of love, Aarzou Khanum talked about the Golden Age of equality still to come, the earthly paradise of sorority and liberty; the peaceful, permanent Revolution. Her calculated appearance was just a gilded theatrical mask. And much of the money from those novels – she was a big seller at the time – came to our cells, paid for rescue operations. So when I was caught – and forced to take the rap for so many others, though I knew less than most of them – I protected her above all. I rotted in solitary confinement in Lahore Fort for three months. If it hadn't been for old Pandit Jawaharlal getting me off – owed my father a favour, you know – I'd have been flayed. Her husband came to me in my cell before I left. It was there that he told me how his wife, in a moment of fear for herself, had betrayed me: and I wondered how much she knew, and how she could have known anything at all, because I never had carried a list of conspirators, and there were things that I did not know and would not have told her, in fear for her, if I did. So I thought that she perhaps had always known more than I; and, worse still that she may have been a spy all along.

'And then, all those years later, she writes this poem, telling this story, absolving herself of everything and dumping all blame on me. I could still hardly believe that she – she – would turn me over to that sleazy husband she'd hated after the first years of their marriage, who had forced her to churn out romances and turned her gems into sawdust or tawdry tinsel. And deny her own part in the struggle, her dreams and dawning visions. To turn so viciously against a man who had loved her almost as much as his life and their dream of revolution.

'But it took me years to unravel the mystery. Put this all in your book, for Aarzou's gone and very soon old Agha will be dead, and as for me, my months in prison have ensured that I have nothing left to lose. Shame, honour, home, dreams; I shed all hope's burdens years ago. Yes, put it in your book, and perhaps you and that bright young critic who interrogated me at the Academy should join forces. Your diligence and her ferocity, combined, might produce a worthy book.

'So let me tell you the truth of the last canto of Aarzou's poem. What she may have written, if she'd seen the truth. Maybe she did: only history will reveal that to us. Or maybe she herself destroyed what her intuition must have told her, erased for ever what she finally wrote. More probably, the Agha did it for her.

'But. Let me face you with my version of the story, in dramatic form. I leave it all to you, and time, to judge. So. Listen:

'Three years ago I decided to accept the government's invitation to come home – though Pakistan hardly was my home, for I hadn't lived there more than six years, but I have no other, either. I was feted, lionized, received with acclaim and even love. And then one day old Potiphar – it is the best name for him, I have to admit – turned up at my door. He had once, though somewhat stout, been a fine-looking man; now he was a sickly white, fat as a frog, and walked with an ivory-headed stick. I greeted him with as much courtesy as I could muster.

AGHA (muttering): I owe you an explanation.

YUSUF: We have no debts to settle. Your wife saw to that.

AGHA: Forgive an old man's impatience. But it was my jealousy, my impotence, my fury and my fear for my wife – whom I loved, because she was the Aphrodite who had risen from the foam of my literary dreams, in many ways my creation – that led to your downfall. It was I who found the plans for the assassination. Her name and yours were on a list of intellectuals with Marxist inclinations, Soviet sympathies and shady contacts. She denied nothing; not her wanton fornications with you, my friend and protegée; not her wild revolutionist dreams. Not even her betrayal of the aesthetic I had so painstakingly created for her. But how she begged me to let you go! She even said that she would take the punishment for your deeds. And I told her that after a required punishment I would arrange for your release. Silence – her eternal silence – was what I demanded for the favour. I would save you if she never dabbled with the politics of the revolution again.

She was merely a messenger. A cog in the wheel. But you, with your tiger's eyes and your snake's ways, you crept into my life, availed of my genius, cavorted with my wife: Ah, my friend and my adversary, my rival in life and art, I hated you. I swear, as much and more than I loved you. I wanted you dead; then eventually I realized it was not your death but the living corpse of your shame and exile, dragged through the streets of our city tied naked to a packhorse, that would satisfy me. I wanted, with your admirers, to smell the stench of your defection. So that I could feel the triumph, then, of being your benefactor, the supplicant for your release, the release of a traitor to the nation. The worst crime in our country's eyes. To see you flee, a dissident and defector, into the arms of our enemy. I arranged the evidence which revealed the insignificance of your involvement. I could have destroyed her, too, along with you, but you realise that any word of her involvement in your subversions would have spelt the end of my prestige. I had to protect her to protect myself, and the price I paid her was your freedom. Also, she was my way of living. She was a wonderful writer, as her last verses prove, far greater than you or I. Can you imagine? What a fine reversal! For of course it was I who had the connections – I who betrayed you, but she had the last, dark laugh. She maintains her silence but tells her tale of sorrow and vengeance; steals my victory to take revenge; reveals her adultery in the bargain, shames my manhood, and damns herself as a traitor to love, which she never was. After all, she was my student; and she learned, though painfully, that the end of an old story can never be changed, and life, however dramatic, must be betrayed to create true art. Reality can never yield the joys and sorrows of a life lived intensely, moment by moment, on the virgin page. So in the end, my dear Yusuf, she cheated us both in her fidelity to her art. Kill, lie, maim, steal, even give up living, as she did: but serve the masterwork. That's all there is to live for.

YUSUF: But why the revenge on me? We were collaborators. Travellers on the same road. Our desire for each other was incidental. We saw the same visions.

AGHA: Because I told her you were involved in the assassination plans, of which, I discovered, she knew nearly nothing . . . and then I told her of the plot – which, of course, I invented – masterminded by the Indians and the Russians, to take us over . . .

YUSUF: But she has Yusuf castrated in the story! So heavy a punishment for a secret kept from a woman! I remember well the innocent machismo of those days, in which even the most dedicated revolutionaries, if they were women, were not entrusted with certain secrets . . .

'So you're admitting that you were involved in the conspiracy?' Malik was incredulous.

'I'm not admitting or denying anything', said the poet. 'Let's just say I knew more than some and a lot less than others. But you are taking us away from my story. Listen:

'I said to old Potiphar:

"But castration!"

'And he responded:

"Oh. My fault, I'm afraid. For I also told her that you were a double agent, who had sold our secrets to foreign powers, and then relented and confessed your plots to me. I said, too, that you had toyed with my great love, just as you had trifled with her heart. You should have seen her face. The man for whom she had humiliated herself before the husband she had grown to despise; for whose wretched life she had even been prepared to sacrifice her freedom: Yusuf, the traitor, not only to his land but then again to the cause she had thought he represented. Then perhaps her fears for your life and safety really did turn into a desire for revenge: and she, too, wanted to reveal your ignominies to the world. And so she settles her scores with the two of us: the one she thought had betrayed and sold her dreams, and the one who, by revealing what she thought was the truth, revealed her beloved to her as a traitor."

'I lunged forward; I wanted to hit him, but then it occurred to me that he may even, in the end, have tampered with the climactic verses of Aarzou's masterwork, just as he interfered with our lives and our dreams and with history itself so that he could get her to write the book he wanted. The old devil. She surprised even him. Somehow these thoughts made me laugh, and then I was laughing at the wretched waste of our lives and our passions, and what a great, great comedy of waste it seemed, how we'd grown older and learnt almost nothing, and I was still laughing when the old man went out silently, like the withered phantom of the past that he was.

'Does my tale' – said Yusuf, relighting his cigar – 'answer some of your questions?'

Skies

Four Texts for an Autobiography

The First Sky
Summer, Lake and Sad Garden

Why should I stop, why?
The birds have gone in search
of the blue direction.

Forugh Farrokhzad

I think that we are those people on whom misfortune
has fallen and I am he who is most at fault.

Intizar Husain

August 1996

This is the dream:
There's the man, on a playground – not a painter's impression, just a
dusty patch. He's with his lover, or at least he thinks it's her. And there's
a child, with wild grey eyes and straw coloured hair, leading a band of
other children. He knows the child, but he can't remember who he is. Hal
Mera, his lover says. That's his name. Come here, Hal. The child looks
back at them with a cold fire. Shouts something vicious, crude, at the
man's lover. Then he runs. Angry, the man chases Hal. The child runs
down to where a ladder's propped up against a rocky slope, leading to a
barren field. The sky above is a forbidding grey. Then he's halfway up

the ladder. The man has the child's foot in his hand. Hal's holding on to
a rock. Struggling to get away. I'll kill you, you little bastard, the man
says. But he doesn't know where the anger is coming from, the hot
violence. He's only a child, Hal, though his grey eyes are a mercenary's.

Forget turquoise and the hissing of summer green. And the sea's out
of style this season. The sky and the city and you are draped in grey
dust from dawn till nightfall. But there in the desert landscape you
suddenly see a bright patch of red blooming in the dust. And just as
suddenly the grey refracts a touch of hidden sun. It turns to gold. Even
the dust. Then the darkness falls, like a winding sheet. On such a night
they drove out, down wide new avenues lined by by tall towers of glass
and chrome, through squares enclosing asymmetrical marble
monuments to modernity, past the boating basin with its throngs of
people eating grilled meats at small tables in the cooling night breeze,
to a lane bathed in purple. The smell of salt and the sea wind hung
over their heads. Against a purple-black horizon that seemed quite
close there were long, long bands of icy white. He turned to Zoya and
asked: Are those bands of salt? Come on Sameer, she said. It's surf.
Can't you see the waves coming at us? So that's my sea, he thought. I
thought they'd chased it away from here.

Karachi, star of the sands, jewel of the green Arabian Sea . . .

They'd built an amusement arcade on reclaimed land not far away
in Clifton, near the ancient shrine. Carloads of young men in tight
jeans and flower-laden girls dressed in their mothers' old saris in
imitation of Indian filmstars cavorted here late into the night. He sat
on a wall from which you would once have seen the sea at high tide
and the sand at low. Now there were ferris wheels. Ribboned in blue,
yellow and red. There he talked about Hal Mera and his violent,
unexpected fury. And about that other recurring dream: He's standing
on a stage, prepared. It's a grand performance, a special occasion. And
suddenly his lines are all gone. His lover – or at least he thinks it's her
– is prompting him from the wings. But it's no good. He can't go on;
he's stammering. He walks off the stage in shame. I can't, he stutters.
I just can't.

— That's when I started stammering, Sameer said. I just couldn't speak English any more. Who was the child? And why did he take my tongue away? And why isn't there any blue left here after the miles I've travelled to find it? And why am I still stammering?

— All I know is that those dreams brought you here, Zoya said in response. Hal Mera? Haal Mera. The state you're in. In an English accent. Stop looking for the past. It's gone from here.

That was the only time he saw the sea that summer.

∾❀∾

But then there was also the walk to the old house. They were on a faintly-lit street lined with low trees. He felt he knew some of the houses there, but when he wanted to turn down the familiar lane that would lead him home, the street seemed to have come to an end, and there were no more lights beyond that corner.

— There were two little lakes here. One on either side of the road. One was blue and one was green. They used to call the green one the maneater. We used to wade in the blue one. They built a park around it later.

— Let's turn back, Zoya said. You've made a mistake. The lake's been dead for years. It's a garbage-dump. We're in the wrong place.

He didn't speak; just grabbed her hand and turned left into the darkness.

— We're here, he said. I told you I'd find it.

And there it is, the lane he remembers, flooded in white light: the old house barely changed, the low walls around the sunken garden barely changed, the tall proud coconut palm he'd looked at from his window now leaning to one side and strapped to a wall, the jasmine bushes stripped away. Changed but recognizable. Still there. Like our relationship with remembrance: Light suddenly floods forgotten corners, darkness envelops places once so bright. And sometimes we're fortunate enough for time to bring us back to stare our dreamscapes in the face.

At his lecture the next day he said:

— We probably all live in three rooms at once: the room of memories, the room of dreams and the room of our chore-burdened present. And that's the attic, crowded with the debris and the phantom toys of the other rooms. Being a migrant is something like that, too: only more complex, because we inhabit about as many houses as well; but our continuities are shattered and even words play games with each other as memories suffer the distortions of other languages. We become, to quote an Indonesian writer, cultural stammerers. (Take me, for example: I read the world from right to left, though I find it hard, sometimes, to decipher the right-to-left passages of my mother tongue. But a web of Arabic letters, in invisible ink, underlines my sentences, forms a palimpsest, crosses and recrosses and mutilates the words I write. Sometimes I feel I write English from right to left.) Perhaps the only difference between those of us who write and the rest of you is the amount of time we spend locked up in our little attic, reckoning with the decor and the embellishment of the other rooms.

— Chic expatriate nonsense, thundered a veteran Hindu communist from Sind. Here we're struggling with our children turning to one or another sectarian party. Or various separatisms.

— But I think I was meant to talk about language, exile and the imagination, Sameer said. I teach literature, not ideologies.

— Go home to your smart university then, the communist said before the dumbstruck chairman silenced him.

Sameer hadn't returned just to search for the house or decipher his dreams. Or then perhaps he had. The story he'd written about his childhood city had come out here to some recognition. But the other project, the book he'd come to launch, was the official reason for his visit. Two years in the planning, six months in the writing. And no end to the problem of working on a social history of fiction that some –

including his editor – felt was arcane, conservative and politically irrelevant. Others saw it as a work of impeccable scholarship, a tribute to language and heritage. After all, it was his doctoral thesis from one of those western universities people here respected so much. The recently-established Allama Iqbal Academy Press, funded by the World Council of Muslim Intellectuals, had offered for it while it was still in its thesis stage. The word Muslim was enough to set the ears of certain local *litterateurs* and self-appointed secular arbiters of the nation's conscience on fire, but others, including Zoya, gave him some grudging support.

— Don't you feel we've advanced at all since the turn of the century? he was asked by editors and journalists alike at an informal press-conference in the post-modern coffee bar of a hotel which was the haunt of radical and impecunious writers who debated the day's issues over very expensive cups of tea.

He was watching on a video monitor the antics of a singer who looked like a smart clerk in a mirror-encrusted Sindhi jacket. To the robust accompaniment of a brass band with a particularly raunchy tenor saxophonist playing a local folksong, the boy was raising thin fingers like a dozen little earthworms above his head and writhing his jean-clad hips.

His answer, distracted and lame, was that the occurrence of one *fin de siècle* demanded an examination of another.

— But what about the riots, the terrors, the ethnic conflicts we've known lately, here in this very city to which you once belonged? they asked.

— The swans have flown, and the crows and the caravans of camels have left the deserts, and now only loves' name remains in the burning sand, sing allahallahallah, sang the clerk on the video monitor in a voice piercing and sweet as a teenage girl's.

— The city I belonged to has become invisible now, Sameer said. Only its ghosts and its shadows remain.

He was reminded of an incident in his childhood. His mother and their neighbour would take turns to drive the children of both households to school. One day their neighbour, hit by the driver of the car in front of him, had got out of his own car on the crowded bridge that connected Victoria Road to Clifton, dragged the perpetrator of the accident by the collar to the street, and created a traffic jam while he punched the little swarthy proletarian's ears and nose until he bled. When Sameer got to school, late, he was ostracized by his entire class. Even his friendly Parsi desk-mate Spenta moved away to sit alone in the dark corners of the back of the classroom. Later, during recess, his Goan teacher Mrs Menezes told him the cause: He'd been part of an incident in which a white man had beaten up a native and a poor man at that. Somehow, he'd let down the side; as if he'd touted for an alien cricketer, say Gary Sobers, at a match. (But Gary was a dark man from the Queen's Commonwealth, which muddled matters slightly.) Colonial times were over, Mrs Menezes remarked, but these white wretches still stalked around like rulers. Sameer, who'd never yet spared a thought (his ten years spent in a polyglot city) for skin colour or nationality, now realized that – of course – kind, gruff Schneider was American. White, or rather red, and identical in appearance to the rough Englishmen still remembered by older locals. And today – there are small groups of gun-bedizened youths lolling against walls, cigarettes hanging from pursed lips. Self-styled vigilantes, nostrils twitching for trouble like dogs for bitches on heat. The rich ride in armoured cars. *Since the Afghan war, we've become an arms dump, a drug dump, a city beseiged. Blame Uncle Sam. We sold our souls and when the cold war was over the rednecks flushed us down the drain.* That's what his friends say. And he retorts, when are we finally going to learn? Stand up to them. Take your own responsibility. Find yourselves a half-honest leader.

Don't speak in the first person, he tells himself each moment. Your pronouns get mixed up halfway through your phrases.

— Times have changed since my days here, he told a journalist ruefully. (They were seated on the roof terrace of a house not far from the neighbourhood he'd grown up in. Smells of night-blooming flowers mingled with smoke and the indefinable odour of lanes. Illicit gin was flowing over ice and slices of tart green lime. There was a power failure, but the light of a misty half moon lit up their discussions.) There's a city of dust and squatter's shacks I don't recognize, by the side of our city of illusions and bright lights. Once we were all Pakistani. United against the power of the intruder. I didn't even know that I belonged to the Sunni majority till I was eight. Or, indeed, that Sunnis were a majority. Now we're at each other's throats, using sects and dialects to create spurious causes. I don't know what to say because I condemn violence and I fail to understand the reason why there should be carnage instead of peaceful debate. I can't say whose side I'm on because I'm only on the side of the peacemakers.

On a wall beyond, a poster freshly painted in red proclaimed:

OUR FATHERS SHED RIVERS OF THEIR OWN BLOOD TO COME TO THIS LAND. THIS IS OUR ONLY COUNTRY NOW. OUR GOLDEN LAND. WE, TOO, ARE CHILDREN OF THE INDUS RIVER.

The second book for which he's just signed a contract with AIAP – the one his university will probably give him a sabbatical to research, and a very decent grant – is concerned, once again, with the past. Though a personal past, this time. His mother's uncle Aman had been a very fine writer; he'd found out about this just by chance, when his mother – on a cold, cold afternoon in a Greenford semi-detached to which he'd taken her by tube and minicab – was talking to an old friend of hers, Annie Q, a renowned novelist who'd lived and written for many years in Karachi after Partition, and then returned to India. She was narrating a traditional ballad. A tribal chieftain's wife begs him to bring her a string of legendary pearls that belong to a powerful prince's wife. She threatens to leave him for the King's harem if he doesn't fulfil her desire for the jewels. The chieftain holds up the lady's caravan and, bandit-like, makes off with the precious loot. Intrepid as a robber, the chieftain, also a fool like many of the courageous, doesn't have the guile to cover his tracks; he's hunted down, he confesses his crime. My lady asked for the pearls and I did what I did for love, he says. The prince responds: God and the King love the man who tells the truth. They let him go.

— I know the story, Annie Q said. It has a tragic end in the version I know, though. The Queen's brother has him arrested and imprisoned again. He sends his wife the jewels and says: May these replace the youth you'll now surrender to a widow's life. It was written as a long story in a beautiful collection of tales called *The Teardrop*.

— So you know my uncle Aman's work? his mother asked. He died so young, I thought he'd been forgotten. Virtually at the start of his career. And I don't even have a copy of his book . . .

— It's been out of print for years, Annie said. But you have to realize he was one of his time's leading literary lights. And wasn't there some terrible scandal around his death? He and the writer Afkar were both in love with the same woman and they made a suicide pact. Afkar lived – became a ghastly bureaucrat. Aman died. Betrayed. I think there was a touch of skullduggery.

Sameer's mother went white and said nothing.

. . . Flash back to another August. Last year.

He's waiting outside a little guesthouse in Islamabad for someone he doesn't know: Zoya Zamaan, who's translating parts of his dissertation to include in a volume she's editing, *The Forgotten Women Writers of Pakistan*. Over the blue-green silhouette of hills in the distance hangs an orange-red globe that could be either sun or moon; with a good sense of direction, he might have been able to tell. But then it's difficult to make out anything in this new town.

The August breezes felt almost cool. It had drizzled all day, but now the sky had opened a huge golden eye. An ambulance drew up. A tiny woman in white shalwar-qamiz, with a waterfall of silky hair cascading over her crushed white dopatta, tumbled out. She extended a hand to take his firmly and introduced herself. It emerged, in conversation, that she divided her time between running a division of the local Health Authority, and writing in various genres.

Zoya had started her career as a celebrated romantic poet, taught by her male mentor – himself famous for his espousal of progressive causes – to observe the Boundaries of the Heart. But at the age of twenty she strayed into the territory of savage social satire in her verses, then she wrote an elegy after the national disgrace of the Bangladesh war. She earned the censure of erstwhile flatterers. She soon made a public statement to the effect that all poetry today – even the supposedly political – was dust and ashes, written by geriatrics and aspiring bureaucrats. Women poets merely fulfilled drooling senile male fantasies. She took up radical reportage instead. But as more than half her targeted audience – the country's disenfranchised women – was illiterate, she reached them through the medium of entertainment most popular with the proletariat, the teledrama, fulfilling the irrepressible urge that only the shadowplay of word with image could satisfy in her. She was prolific in her production of scripts for prime-time soaps with women's issues at the core of their rather scandalous narrative complexities, combining the expected escapist romance with reformist messages. Rather in the manner of those irrelevant early novelists you're so fond of and insist on writing about, she'd later delight in telling Sameer. She had left Karachi in a rage about the deteriorating relationship between communities and massive evidence of resulting police brutality. The journal she had run singlehandedly there had been targeted by several oppositional groups, with bomb threats, menaces and hate mail directed at its drive towards communal harmony. Religious conservatives had also condemned – for its disregard of moral values – a short play she'd written about a woman choosing to terminate a pregnancy that, under the law, could jeopardize her pending divorce from a violent and domineering second husband. It was a portrait of Zoya's own first marriage.

. . . Present tense. Again.

Zoya's come back to Sameer's native city: she left Islamabad a few months after their first meeting. She's set up a new publishing company, an NGO that foregrounds feminist concerns but also highlights obscure and valuable aspects of national culture. She decided she'd taken a coward's way out by running away from Karachi; she could only deal with her problem by confronting it. She's a confrontational woman.

Her frequent pronouncements about the ambiguous position of migrant intellectuals seem to imply that Sameer, the archetypal expatriate scholar, is in flight from his past here; but he, too, she realizes, is unable to stay away. One of her first publishing projects is to be the Urdu translation of his dissertation. It is at her behest, that he came here to launch the book she'd encouraged him to complete and is still busy translating. His obsession with cultural history though (she suggests) is also an escape; a quest for a lost moment of innocence and optimism in a patriotic Neverland.

He finds it hard to explain that his is a fascination with the dying throes of dreams. What are we, he reflects in his journal one night, but a single tear, frozen into a bell of glass that chimes the music of its own destruction? And isn't a poem, a painting, a prayer or a piece of writing nothing but a vain attempt to gather fragments of glass when the bell of our bodies is shattered by the sound of its own weeping?

But Zoya and he, from the start, have got on surprisingly well. Her political correctness, compounded of socialism, feminism and a dedication to the plight of ethnic minorities, is undercut by a mad, subversive sense of humour and the sound and detached aesthetic that makes her so fine a polemicist, poet and editor. She believes greatly, too, in the translator's craft, which she sees, to Sameer's surprise, as an art – but then she's a woman who sees little difference between artists and artisans. If, in conversation, her attitudes err towards the ardent and judgemental, her writings and her critical finesse overturn her zeal, balance her fervour. Her comments on his research were, at first, occasionally patronizing, though he soon became aware that it was the time and period he was chronicling, and its reformist zeal, of which she was dismissive, not his methodology or approach.

She also loves fancy food, and many of their debates took place over the cosmopolitan delicacies – Japanese, Afghan, Italian – that the seaside city provided. They were eating in one of those restaurants that seemed to be everywhere in the chic new neighbourhood called Zamzama, glass menageries with exotic menus perused by luminous young matrons lunching with teenage sons or liaising with them on vodaphones propped on elegant shoulders, when she'd proposed – over a heaped bowl of green ribbon pasta succulent with chicken, cream and mushrooms bearing little resemblance to any dish he'd savoured in Italy – that he write another book.

— The elegance of your style, she said, your passion for language and its vagaries, raises your writing above the level of academic research. It carries its own significance and conviction, transforming critical discourse and historical anecdote into subjective art.

The conversation veered, as it always did, to the legacy and the state of the nation. Suddenly the image of Annie Q and his mother in that Greenford salon came to him. But it wasn't the delicacy of Aman's visions, known to him only in his mother's lyrical versions, that he cited; it was the moment in which Aman – a moment duly recorded in his one essay that survived the short blaze of his life – had left for Pakistan after Partition.

— He didn't belong to the Muslim League, or to any other party. He was in Delhi, a lecturer at a university, when a friend of his warned him that sectarian zealots had marked his door with a great white swastika. The friend spirited him out of a window, draped in a woman's black veil, and put him on the next chartered Dakota to Pakistan. You didn't need a ticket or a passport in those days. So he found himself in Lahore, a city completely alien to him, against his will. Shortly after that, he moved to Karachi. He remained an isolated romantic. He didn't join the Progressive Writers Association . . .

— But he adopted this country as his own with a passion . . . he wrote so many stories about the incomers and the tragicomedy of Partition . . .

— Do you have his book?

— No, but I know someone who might. Have you come across Nadim Zahidi?

— I know his work.

— Talk to him. He'll point you in the right direction so you can retrieve all sorts of archival papers. What I really like about his work is the identification with his new land. And when you think of what they do to us now – do you remember when Ayub told us Mohajirs – so-called refugees – that if we didn't like what was happening to us at that time – I was about thirteen – we could just walk into the deep blue sea? Well, it seems neither sea nor sky wants us any more. Oh, this state we're in.

Zoya's family had come to Karachi from Dhaka in 1951, the year before she was born. They'd left their home in Patna at Partition. Her real surname was Siddiqui and Siddiquis were once, she said when in cynical mood, low-caste Hindu weavers.

— Hooch-makers, I've heard, which is worse, Sameer retorted late one evening in Clifton, waiting to be served at a fast-food bar that served several varieties of biryani. At least you're not a tanner. Nor a horse-trader like my lot.

— Pale-skinned horse-traders, she said, who rode across the borders from foreign lands. Makes all the difference to our lot. We still think in terms of caste. Look at our Christians, poor souls. The untouchables have the finest church which the Catholics won't attend because they converted from higher Hindu castes.

— But my people . . . my grandfather's grandfather was brought up by a dyer and had to work at his trade for a while, so they say . . .

— Haven't you ever thought of writing about your Sindhi family instead of Aman? Now there's an idea for your third book . . .

— It's already been done. In Sindhi. All you need is to get a translation. Which I can't do.

Though Sameer had a working knowledge of Siraiki and Punjabi, his Sindhi was not even functional. But Zoya chattered away in several local languages; she'd married and divorced a doctor who'd worked in the interior of the Sind, and her children's Sindhi was as fluent as their Urdu and as their Sky TV-inspired Ameringlish. For people like Zoya , India held no loved or loving memories, no sensations of loss or yearning. It was a foreign country, to be enjoyed, on a holiday, simply as that. For years she – and people like her – had ignored the growing sense of nation as alienation that was being imposed, quite artificially, upon them. Then taunts, factions and politics of the blood, soil and native son variety had forced them to search for a third solution, which often made them espouse positions that occasionally appeared mutually contradictory. Sameer, who was born and brought up here and had long, deep roots in Sind and the northern region, had always despised ethnic separatism. And yet the pain he felt from people like her – coming at him like the smell of fenugreek or fried onions – made him feel sorry, not to say guilty, about the sturdiness of his claims to this soil. On the other hand, his mother's people were still in India, and he travelled freely to that country. Some of his most passionate memories still breathed beneath Indian skies. Often, on this trip, he would find himself voicing stances as contrary, as confused as those that echoed around him.

❧❀❧

The seed of his new project, sown over a meal of green pasta with Zoya, germinated under her green thumb. But he began to discover that what he was planning, far from being a critical study or even the biography expected by the AIAP, was a new selection of his uncle's stories, prefaced and placed in context by a long piece he'd write. AIAP could publish the English versions with a biographical introduction; Zoya would produce the Urdu version of the book for him. He envisaged it as a sequence of song-like fragments, a caravan of images of travellers in grief and joy, multiple migrations, cross-pollination and seed dispersal. Crossings from Iran and Iraq and Afghanistan and Uzbekistan. Some members of his mother's Indian family had mixed their blood with craggy Pathans and mild-mannered Sindhis here. He's a product of such a union. His uncle's story will be one of such crossings, ending, perhaps, in his mother's story and his own: an epilogue in which the stories of the past live on, in rented flats in Greenford.

He travelled around Pakistan on that trip, but he didn't go back to Karachi. The sky and the sea were calling out to him: We are not for you. This state we're in. You've left us to our troubles. Now go back to your own. And he did. To the lengthy hours of his new lectureship and the disaster of separations. To the city where slimy drops running down drainpipes remind you that happiness is a dirty word.

But look at him now. Here he is, again. Surrounded by scattered dreams of lost turquoise and summer green. Back, once more, to dreams of the city at the sea's edge. The story of Uncle Aman is relegated, unfinished, to a drawer.

Late one night, on the tube, after an evening class and a reception, he thinks: At least I should write a story of homecomings and leavetakings. About love and partings and a poet, perhaps.

He makes a list on the back of an envelope.

HIBISCUS DAYS:
1. The futility of writing.
2. A few drops of absence on a page.
3. Colours lost in summer, lake and sad garden.
4. White sea, unshed, behind your eyes.
5. On your lips this other salt.
6. So many skies to choose from. Calling you away, alone, towards your own stretch of blue.

The Second Sky
Hibiscus Days

These tarnished rays, this night-smudged light
This is not that dawn for which, ravished with freedom,
we had set out in sheer longing,
so sure that somewhere in its desert the sky harboured
a final haven for the stars, and we would find it.

Faiz Ahmed Faiz

Jaisalmer April 1984

Dear M.:

Anochecer. The night, falling on sand still gleaming, now white, now blue. From my window I watch it pass. *Amanecer.* The dawn, red, and the sand almost like water now. (Mirages? Or my tired eyes?) These Spanish verbs for changing times, so apt in Rajasthan. It is April. I am alone. At night, on a train from Jodhpur to Jaisalmer, I saw the rising moon reflected in a ditch full of yellow water. I was restless. I rose and took my book of poems – I was reading Faiz in Urdu yet again – into the corridor. I crouched, face at window-level, longing for air. I felt a movement behind me, heard a voice, turned around. It was the attendant. He offered me a folding chair, tea from a flask. Began to talk.

— You belong here. You're on your way home.

(Not, of course, strictly true. But I'm not about to tell him that. Better to belong here for a night.)

— I'm going to Jaisalmer, I said. After ten years.

— That's where I come from.

I could tell. Words, faint cadences of his native village, lemon-sharp on his tongue. I, too, have picked up the accents of these regions by the border, half-forgotten dialects.

Hours went by, it was nearly dawn, we saw the sun rise. I gave him whisky from the duty-free bottle I'd brought for hospitalities, shared

Marlboros from my soft pack. He asked about my life in London, about my return to India, about my travels. I told him about you, that I was on my way to look for you.

— When I was nineteen, he said, I married the girl my parents chose. I didn't know her. Two years later she gave birth to our child, a daughter. For months I didn't touch her. Somehow I thought she was sacred, touched by a god. I spent months at a time in Delhi or on the road. I rarely saw her. A day or two at a time. Then, one day, a hot day, I was lying on my string bed shirtless. A woman came to my room. A strong woman who lived in my compound, the wife of one of my mates on the railroad. They'd told me she wanted me. Her husband was older. Didn't care what she did. I was half-naked. Without a word she began to touch me, climbed on my bed, kissed my shoulders, my chest, my face, ran her hands over and over my face, through my hair. She touched my thighs. I'd never known a fire like that. Knowing a woman's touch makes the months of lack longer, harder, the moment of bodies meeting more urgent. I loved her so fiercely that time. Then again. I'd never taken my wife like that, like I took her. Then afterwards, when I saw my wife, guilt and shame struck me. But seeing her again, being with her, the mother of my child, filled me with a tenderness far beyond words, bigger than anything I've known, than I'll ever know. I lay beside her, night after night, touching her gently, breathing in her smell, never taking her. My penance, it was, and my joy. It came to me, then, that the love you bear for a stranger, a newcomer in your life, not bound to you by flesh or blood, is greater than the love you have for your parents or your child. A love born of your choice, of joy, of flying together like birds in search of water. When I went back to Delhi, when the other came again and again to my bed, I knew that the fire in my belly was nothing, was ashes, compared to the love I had for my wife. I knew that I could give myself, again and again, in loneliness or despair, to another, take a woman's careless offerings, but my love for my woman had become my whole life. When I'm with her I give her all of me. When I'm away I love her more. I carry her with me wherever I go, my beloved burden.

... *Anochecer. Amanecer.* In those hours of darkness turning into hours of light, in my room in Jaisalmer, watching the changing colours of the ocean of sand, I search for the lost music of my travelling companion's words in the foreign language in which you and I, my childhood companion, write to each other. The songs of our mothers remain like echoes in our skulls, lost on the wind of our longings like birds with broken wings or grains of sand in a storm, never to find written shapes and forms. But listen carefully to the melody between the lines: you'll hear their echoes there.

Your letter was waiting for me here. What a mistake: I'd thought your body was a map of my journey's longing, that to lay my head on your shoulder with my mouth on your clavicle would be my homecoming. *Ye na thi hamari qismat ke visal-e-yar hota* ... But, to rephrase Ghalib, we were not friends, nor fated to meet.

Accept my congratulations. You'll understand that I've changed my plans. It's best if we don't see each other for a while. How strange it seems: to be so close to a frontier I won't cross. The sand on either side of the barriers is the same. I've got my visa but I won't come to Karachi for the celebrations. This is my last letter to you. It's written in sand. I'm not sure that I'll even write it down. Maybe the desert wind will carry it to you across the border. But here's a poem, my gift from the dunes:

Hibiscus days,
walking from desert to desert:
here in this place I've become
another, at home among dunes
I've never seen before.
Twisted by a gesture of history,
I've found my source:
these sands, these stones,
white skies and winds are my home.
Come, sand, burn my skin black:
you'll recognize me. Give me back

the colour of my desert ancestors,
darkness surging through my faded
parchment. Come, sky, pour your wine
into my empty sockets, give your gold
to my tongue: you will see me.
Absence, beat your wings within me,
deep: I will want you more.

Like the silver cities built
upon the ruins of the cities
of gold my nomad fathers sacked,
like golden cities swallowed
by their own decay, the citadel
of my past is disintegrating.
Stones piled one upon another,
walls, structures and sanctuaries,
stones of history and fable,
waiting for their saviour. Like
their fallen images of brass
or bronze, effigies of deities
and heroes, pieces of my past
still beckon: a perfect arm,
a broken hand, a neck, a foot,
a soulless smiling face.
No sculptor to remake them,
no writing hand to mould them
into language.

Born between the desert
and the sea, a child of dust,
I ask: Do boundaries concern me?
Borders exist? Are grains of sand,
like currencies, stamped
with slogans and identities?

A wanderer, I see the cities
I dishonour as mirages, mirror-
images of cities in the sand.
A stranger to tall trees, to hills,
to mists and mountain-fogs
and valleys, I'm a foreigner
in places that lay claim to me.

But these gates you never should
unlock, they cast their shadows
here, of places you never can
reenter or regain. So, my friends,
don't search for me. But if you
know, just send a message in
a gypsy's song:
How are things in our city?
Do your children still run
to the gates, when vagrant
musicians, passing by, play
the songs of our companions
from the inlands on their pipes?
Do they still tremble when
the music of the flute invites
them to the border? Does jasmine
still fill the air with its
singing, calling to the rain?
And your senses – are they full
of the mad smell of the earth's
thirst? Do your feet yearn, in
answer to the call to dance,
or do they – as ours still do -
restrain themselves,
your dancing feet
your clapping hands?

My feet on the sand
are still silent.
Gipsies in the distance
play a note on one string.
Take my hands now, friends,
take all of me. Before
I go on. And remember
when you think of me
and the deep colours
of your hibiscus days

: The salt drops of my words
falling, falling on these
letters, like the first rain
on our parched land.

The Third Sky
Requiem for a Lost Father

. . . Indeed this is nothing new. This narrow path has been trod
many a time already, it's only that this time the journey is one to
mark the way.

Pramoedya Ananta Toer

Suddenly, the sand
has turned to gold.
A mirage lies ahead, yet again.

Perveen Shakir

London March 1998

Dear A:
No, you're right: there were no separations. I came back to no

relationship, nobody serious in my life for me to separate from. And of course I only made one trip back to Pakistan.

A few months before visiting, after an absence of nearly twenty-eight years, the city of my birth, I'd met a couple at a dinner here in London. She, very pregnant now, had worked as a senior editor for an international publishing company; he, soft-spoken and urbane, was an expatriate historian who'd gone home with his doctoral thesis under his arm to get it published and been assigned to her editorial surveillance. He had found a job as a teacher at a school for privileged boys in Lahore; she worked in Karachi. But they'd fallen in love and decided to marry, and returned to London, where they now lived, in a ground floor flat in a condominium on the Isle of Dogs.

I was struck by sentimental notions. I remember announcing, on my forty-first birthday, that I was going to write two love stories. One would be based on their romance. The other was a story taken from my own life – a love unwritten, a text abandoned nine years ago.

I was already planning to come to Karachi that summer. I can't remember if Sameer's dreams, which of course were really mine, inspired me to make the long-delayed return journey to the home that existed only in my mind; I don't even know, they might have come later, when I was already back here and still stammering. Anyway, while I was in Pakistan or when I came back to my London life, the planned love stories flowed into one and became part of the memoir-cum travelogue I knew I wouldn't be able to write. I think I wanted to write about the return of the prodigal: Sameer finding love and fulfilment in his homeland, but not, perhaps, in his city at the sea's edge. Let him fall in love and discover, instead of reclaiming his lost city, the new landscapes of a nation in flux. Throw in his lot, as a prodigal come home, with his compatriots.

I started work on 'Skies' in – September, was it? But there was a problem. In my draft, with its nebulous and fluctuating span of time, Zoya had already returned to Karachi at the story's start: she'd left Islamabad for reasons referred to in the flashback which described their first meetings. I wasn't ready to explore my feelings about

Karachi. Or to set a story in a city I'd only revisited for less than a month as an expatriate celebrity. It seemed voyeuristic to observe and report on the emotions of people who'd been suffering on either side of the hostile divide when I had so often responded to their dilemma by wanting to maintain an equal distance from both. But I had to bring Sameer back to Karachi, excluding the possibility of settling him into a comfortable romance in the city of bureaucrats. The Islamabad connection, though, had given me fresh ideas.

While I was there, that fishbowl city – with its long, long strikes, its mile-wide diatribes against Benazir and her corrupt regime – was still in mourning for a poet I shall not name. She had died a few days after her forty-second birthday, nearly two years before my visit. (I was nearly forty-two, as I wrote.) A bus had run into her car. She was named after a constellation. If, in her lifetime, her graceful verse had turned her into a legend and a heroine, her death had made her into myth. She'd got herself a lot of enemies, with her sexual glamour and her supposedly conformist, anti-political attitudes. She, too, like my Zoya, was a Mohajir; she, too, was from Karachi – she was born there, delivered by the gynaecologist who had been responsible for me. Her poems – unlike those of her older peers – were entirely free of concerted protest. But, when I read the eulogistic biography a friend of hers had written along with a selection of her occasional prose, I became aware that hers were the politics of conscience. There are two kinds of political writing. One adopts the voice of the victim as nervous fingers beat, in accompaniment, the hollow drum of gender and ethnic identity. The other, like Annie Q's, echoes the voice of conscience, veiling shrill cries in whispers, relinquishing the triumphalism of the single message. I had seen Zoya's as the first sort – brilliant technically, with beauty transcending the polemic that inspired her to write. But the dead poet's lesson made me revise my plot. What if Zoya, too, in spite of her fierce ideological stance, was a poet – or prose-writer – of discretion and discernment, who'd written a work the conservatives considered subversive and obscene? One changed sentence could make the city of my birth her native city too;

a mere paragraph could kill her. Sameer's return would be blighted by her death. His research into the past would limp its way into the present as he tried to uncover the truth of her passing. Which, of course, I envisaged as an assassination. Her mouth had got her into trouble with fanatics. They'd done away with her. Sameer would play the amateur detective.

The star-poet's interviews had revealed her admiration for a male celebrity – an actor, let's say, who'd once bared his buttocks on television. He'd returned home from across the black water, repelled by the fleshpots of the western world after many years abroad, in search of the pure waters of home, seeking a house for his unhoused soul. He was now, it was openly reported, poised for political power, in league with obscurantist right-wing forces. While she was also said to have expressed private sympathy for a rebel Mohajir leader and his cause.

What if my Zoya – during her self-exile in Islamabad – had fallen in love with that very handsome celebrity who was, after all, her own age?

What if she had been exterminated, as a political threat, by the paranoia of his party – or, for that matter, by the increasingly minatory policies of the opposition leaders who were courting her?

My projected romance was inclining towards a genre I'd never attempted before: the political thriller or mystery.

Then the 'long hours of the new lectureship' – teaching history and literature – stopped me from working on my story. And, as usual, elements of reality took over, reminding me of that hoary truism: Life is always more dramatic than fiction. So I put aside for a while – not consciously, not deliberately – the stories of Sameer and Zoya, Sameer's work-in-progress on Aman. As for Nadim, I never even got round to giving him a face, a form.

But I couldn't deal with the ethnic conflicts, the political fears, the obsession with nationhood, the mistrust of expatriates, the sense of desperation that are your daily sustenance. Maybe I didn't want to admit that they were too remote from my troubles, I was too distant now from them and the sky and the sea that had said they were not for me. Perhaps I had my own, unique obsessions. How embarrassing it is! to discover unfinished manuscripts and to confess to others (even to yourself) that you don't remember the destinies you'd mapped out for the hapless victims of your imaginings.

But I just couldn't kill Zoya. And I couldn't superimpose on her familiar features the face of the pretty star-poet. So the mystery story I was plotting was abandoned. And were I to resume the romance, I didn't feel it was right to bring Zoya to live in exile here in London: if she came, it would merely be on sabbatical, I'd have to send her home.

The fragment entitled 'The First Sky' ends with the implication that Sameer leaves behind the troubles in his land to return to his own in London. And then the dreams take him back to Karachi, where Zoya's with him by the sea and at the house. I'd planned to keep him there with her, at least for a while. What then? A separation?

The chronology of my fragment is blurred. And, as I've admitted, I hadn't separated from anyone. But let me fill you in, sparingly, on some of the subsequent events of my own life, and where they differ from, or sometimes mirror, those I'd attempted to portray.

There never was a Zoya. That valiant editor, envisaged at times as a dark, massive Amazon and at others as a tiny firebrand, was only a creation of my heart. I didn't really meet anyone quite like her in Pakistan. So I failed to bring to life the love affair – doomed or otherwise – between her and our old friend Sameer. I thought of introducing a triangle. Her, Nadim and Sameer. She stays behind with Nadim. Sameer goes back to his exile's life and his devotion to his (auto)biographical projects. But that was hard, because it meant Sameer had accepted there was to be no homecoming, and, as you know, I was full of dreams then of coming home to live. Sometimes I was nostalgic for a Sind I'd never known. At others my homesickness evoked the Karachi I had just seen, superimposed over the image of my lost seaside city. Then again at times the right-to-left journey of reading my own language, banished from my daily life, would exhaust me: make my eyes blur, my head reel. Sameer's emotions, and many of his experiences, were, as I hardly need to tell you, mine.

And – as you probably know – I never have written, or even contemplated the writing of, a social history of Urdu fiction. Yes, I've written a few research papers on similar themes: one was the keynote lecture I gave in Islamabad, did you read it? which surfaced a few months later in an American journal; I read out another to an academic audience in Bologna a year after. Only the story about the story about Karachi is true, but even that was published, along with two others, after I left. At least some of my fictions found their home in my homeland.

And at the talk I gave to intellectuals in Karachi I didn't speak about the houses and the rooms of memory. (That was in Sweden, two months later.) I told the radicals assembled of Europe's new nationalisms and of the migrant writer's tight-rope walk between intellectual privilege and racial fear. I tried to make comparisons with our city. In Denmark or Holland or France, I said, our dark skins and soft vowels designate our differences. Here you make refugees of those who resemble you most. I do not understand you. That's when the veteran communist wished me a rapid journey back home to unreality.

So. I was talking about reality overtaking fiction. I abandoned 'Skies' and picked up something I'd written years ago; expanded, revised, reworked it in an attempt to write the Pakistani novel I felt I owed to my roots and to my compatriots. The irony is, I couldn't face setting HIBISCUS DAYS (as it was called) in a place with which I'd lost familiarity. So I invented an imaginary country – the Land of the Crescent. I was putting the final touches to it when a friend who was publishing a story of mine on which I'd worked particularly hard broke the news to me in a fax at dawn last March: 'Yusuf and Zuleikha', inspired by Muslim legend and Persian verse and Thomas Mann, a parable of politics and art, was to be censored for flouting new-fangled religious conventions. I found ways of fighting back. The story, which I'd conceived and written with Pakistani readers in mind, did appear. It was about poets and their destiny. I still don't know what they made of it. (I could have resumed my work on 'Skies' now, feeding truth into fiction: Sameer, the expatriate writer, facing censorship. Or Zoya, instead of dying, the target of ire and censure. Not for writing about matters religious – never that; no, for speaking in the voice of the beleaguered sections of Karachi. Obliquely. But no. I didn't want my fiction to parallel the much-publicized histories of Rushdie and Taslima Nasreen. There are some stories best left to reporters and investigative journalists.)

Ah, yes, before that there was the assassination of Murtaza Bhutto by the police on the streets of my city. Sister Benazir fell from power. I can't remember the month, because the stammering and the dreams had made me spend Christmas 1996 and the first few days of 1997 in hospital after an overdose – deliberate or accidental? take your pick – of sleeping pills. I'd been – literally – dying to come home. In hospital, I wrote three short poems:

i.
Exile
a tear stain on a black page
rain falls on parched sand

ii.
Hibiscus
where will I find you
in red dust, or in dreams?

iii.
Eyes
Raised once to the sun in song
Covered now in hands of desperation

I came back to the flat and spent my winter nights awake, speaking on the telephone till dawn to you and other friends in the city that once was mine and had now disappeared. We made fictitious plans: for me to come back to work and live. The novella on which I worked so hard in the days that followed was rejected by three publishers. That was after the teacup storm about censorship. Reflecting, perhaps, the continuation of stammerings and incomprehensible dreams: Hal Mera, the state I was in. Facing an alien nation.

But there was a memory of my city I'd carried with me. Not from my childhood, no: this was new, from the last trip. On the night before I left Karachi, I'd asked my friends – there were three, two men and a woman, a journalist and two poets – to take me to the old part of the city where, as a child, I'd enjoyed eating food from the wayside stalls. Oh no, say the men, it's a violent, dirty place, full of snipers and terrorists. But we go there: the men stay, cowards, in the car, Zoya leads down into a lane. It's quite late in the evening, probably ten. The streets, lined with shops and stores all selling food or flowers, are crowded: families, men dressed in starched white, women brighter and gaudier, the exquisite children of these streets. The smells of butter and spices mingle with the fragrance of flowers. Children, offspring of gipsy ragpickers from the desert, weave through the throngs with strings of jasmine garlands in their hands, begging us: Please buy the night's last flowers for a few rupees before they wither. Little has changed in twenty years. We join the queue which dissolves immediately when a woman is seen to take her place in it. Zoya, for modesty's sake, has pulled her white dopatta over her hair . For the equivalent of a few pounds we carry away a feast – minced lamb baked tight around strings, layered bread so light it crumbles at your touch, gram-flour fritters soaked in tamarind-scented yoghourt, puddings made of pistachios and almonds and ground rice and cream set in earthen bowls. We share a rice-pudding on the road. I don't want to leave Karachi, don't want to leave here; I want to smell the crowds for hours. So. This is where I'll take my leave of Zoya and Sameer. Leave them eating rice pudding from earthen bowls, standing on the lamplit pavement on Burns Road. There's much left unsaid and no time left to say it, but that's true of all homecomings, leavetakings, partings. Sameer buys a garland of jasmine from a gipsy boy and ties it round Zoya's bare wrist.

April 1998

Dear A,

And there's a footnote to the chronicle of Uncle Aman, whose biography Sameer, in my unfinished story, wants so much to write. Now fiction and reality merge. In early March, just in time for my mother's birthday, a heavy parcel arrives from Karachi: her uncle's book of stories. You, my friend, author of several volumes of stories and later many poems about our beseiged city, to whom I'd spoken of my great-uncle the forgotten writer, had managed, as you promised when I left, to unearth his book from the national archives. You xeroxed the whole volume – about four hundred and fifty pages – to send to me. You say that the work of this forgotten pioneering modernist should be revived. Perhaps my efforts and my blood bond with great-uncle Rafi have something to do with this new-found enthusiasm. So I like to think.

My mother's uncle wasn't called Aman: his name was Rafi Ajmeri. His book was called *Kahkashan* (*The Milky Way*), not *The Teardrop*. He wrote about writers who rewrote their lives or sent messages to lost lovers in their fictions, about impoverished intellectuals who travelled the length and breadth of undivided India – Lahore to Calcutta, Kanpur to Bombay – in search of teaching or writing jobs; he wrote about barriers of privilege and pain.

The conversation between my mother and her friend Annie Q – in real life, the writer Qurratulain Hyder – did take place, and my mother did hum the ballad of Daya Gujar, which Uncle Rafi has retold and also transcribed in his book. But it was in Hounslow, I think, not in Greenford. And the stories of skullduggeries and duels don't come from his quiet life. No, I didn't invent those, either: they belong to the biography – or, rather, the death – of another cousin I never knew, and took place, I think, in Hyderabad Sind, to which some of my mother's relatives migrated after Partition. Of Uncle Rafi I only know that he was, like me, of a melancholy temperament; and though he fell in love he lost the object of his adoration to another. He never married. He died very young: in 1937, a decade before the creation of Pakistan. So he never did see the midwifing of the country of my birth; but it's one of the ironies of our histories that a lamp should be lighted in his name in the land he never knew, the home now of his language.

My mother's father left the state he should have ruled, at least in name, to take charge of Daly College in Indore, so that he could bring up his children in a city, where all of them – boys and girls alike – could have an education. His bride, who travelled with him to Indore from Ajmer, had studied at home. She knew the Persian classics, could recite Rumi by heart, and had written for women's journals before her marriage. She, of course, was Rafi's sister, and told her children many of the stories that Rafi would transform into fiction. My grandparents, who married in 1914, never contemplated crossing the distant border (distant from Indore, but not so far from my grandfather's Kathiawar or my grandmother's Rajasthan) to the land of Muslim dreams, and lived together in Indore for fifty-eight years. Their second born, the eldest of my mother's brothers, like me a teacher of literature, should have been a writer – he taught the joy of English to many younger writers now at work. He has been dead eleven years. He did, almost against his will, like Qurratulain Hyder, migrate. He was warned to escape from Delhi by a Hindu friend at the hostel where he, a young man of twenty-seven at the time independence was declared, and not yet a teacher but a civil servant, was living, because a minatory sign – which my mother says was not a Swastika – had been painted on his door. He took a plane to Pakistan. He was interviewed for the new Civil Service there, but his aristocratic birth and fine education were of little relevance in the new country where people were competing for allotments of refugee property and bureaucratic jobs. They never called him up. He stayed a mere five days, my mother says, secure that the dust would soon settle in his native land. And there he returned, spending his life teaching language and literature all over India, refusing to be, though becoming, in a sense, twice over a Mohajir. He lies next to his parents in Indore, the city of his birth.

My father, too, who was my maternal uncle's age, left India at

Partition. Born in Karachi in 1919, he had lived and studied all over the country, and didn't think of Karachi as home. He was living in Delhi in the summer of '47, and had no real thoughts of leaving. But his aunt sent him an urgent message, to travel to Kashmir where her teenage sons had been holidaying, and bring them safely back to Karachi. Once there, my father was told his home in the new India had been sequestered as evacuee property. So with customary stoicism he accepted his home in the newborn country, and six months after married my mother. (Their wedding celebrations were restricted by the assassination of Gandhi, which had taken place a week before. I never asked my father, who had met all the nationalist leaders of the time, if he had met Gandhi. But my father did recount to me how once, when Gandhi visited the state of which my grandfather was then Prime Minister, the great man was on a fast. To my grandfather fell the duty, which he delegated to my father, of finding strawberries, which was all the Mahatma would allow himself to eat. Strawberries in the desert; water from a stone. An ascetic's feast. And now the tragedy of his killing cast a shadow on my father's wedding festivities.)

My father brought his bride – the beloved youngest daughter of her family – across the water to the city of which he was, after all, a native. As all his children – his three daughters and I, his only son, would be. (Later, when I was a boy, he would tell me: I first saw your mother standing by a fountain. She probably knew I was looking at her. So she'd turned away. I fell in love with her back and her long brown hair. Her braid was bristling.) My mother brought her with a dowry of many songs, which she taught to those children, and she learnt many others, which she transcribed, in her fine Persian hand, in a series of notebooks. (One of the songs she learnt from her migrant teacher, himself a great musician, was the admonition of a woman to her young sister-in-law: Do not go out to play in the rain, she says, the fine young men will follow you home. The song ends in an image, almost disassociated, of convicts grinding millstones, felons hanging from the gallow, men shot down by bullets. Only now, in conversation with my mother, I realize that the maiden forbidden from venturing out to play in the rain represents those rebels who took up arms against the British at various historical junctures: we agree that the song was probably composed by the women of Oudh after the events of 1857, the so-called Mutiny, when the dethroned octogenarian King of Delhi himself had written lilting elegies to the defeated soldiers.)

My mother cultivated orchids in her garden. She used to sing a song to us about a pregnant woman whose husband jumps over a wall into a garden of jasmine and oranges to bring her the fragrant oranges she craves. (I lost, during one of our many moves from home to home and country to country, a picture of my mother, dressed in green, standing by the sea, her face, turned three-quarters to our view, bronzed by the desert sun. Her hair, falling away from its knot, is moist and wavy with salt-water and heat. She's pregnant, heavy and proud; her sari, hitched to knees, accentuates the weight of her burden, her burgeoning belly. I am with her, in her, unborn as yet: Look at me, she says, I am bringing you to birth.) I would always imagine their faces, my mother's and my father's, when she sang the song about the woman and the oranges: and when he brought her the orchids she wanted from Ceylon, it was as if those oranges had become orchids now, in our family's version of the song. Two years later, in 1965, he was stranded, a Pakistani national, in Bombay when the farce that they called a war was performed, and when an unsteady peace was declared he was evacuated and sent far, far away, to Beirut, because no aircraft was making the forty-five minute flight to Karachi. He didn't feel at home anywhere for some years after that. In my memory, then, he, too, becomes a Mohajir of sorts, leaving Pakistan – and the growing strife and discontent in the lands he loved with a passion second only to the love he had for his family – to spend most of thirty years in England, where he had studied at Magdalen as a lad and which he left when war was declared in '39; where all but one of his grandchildren were to be born.

But Pakistan was Naomi to my mother's Ruth: she threw her arms around its neck and was the last of us to leave. To this day she won't let go. Fonder, her Ruth-like heart keeps growing, as absence spreads its wings which time has turned from grey to white. (A few days ago I asked her: Mama, isn't it strange that you and Bangladesh took leave of Pakistan in the same year? No coincidence, that, she replied. There were photographs of Yahya feasting the night the war on the East was declared. Nero, I said, you fiddle while your city burns. I decided I'd leave that day.) My mother left her flowers behind in Karachi, and many of her books, including illustrated volumes of *The Bride's Book of Beauty* and *The Lady of the Lotus*, and, of course, the original edition of *Kahkashan*, Uncle Rafi's only collection of tales. Other possessions, including her red wedding sari, pictures of her children as infants, and all but one of the songbooks, were lost in transit.

And look at me now, become dry-eyed dirge singer at my father's grave, lamenting, tears unshed, the severing at his passing of so many links – to my childhood and the house and garden I last saw bathed in light; to dreams of a new country and a long-deferred homecoming; to relics of the princely past of which he was so proud, to which I'm merely connected by drops of blood; to the desert legends and the blood-stirring ballads of Sind which I never learned to sing; to the many, many dead we never were to see again and mourned together; even, ultimately, to the friends in his city who discovered me through my writing and claim me as companion and compatriot. Above all I lament not having said goodbye and all I never, now, can learn from him. I can no longer listen to the gut-wrenching voice of Abida Parvin, the singer I came to know through him, or read the verses of the songs she sings: songs by the old poets – Shah Abdul Latif and Sachal Sarmast, Bulley Shah and Khwaja Ghulam Farid – who sang in places he knew well, Mithankot and Bhit Sharif and Uch. Now my father's country is to me, like my mother's India before, a beloved absence. As he, too, is. He died suddenly. He didn't want a slow death. His heart stopped beating, my sister told me at eleven o'clock one particularly cold December night, four or five hours after I had last seen him. We remembered then that he had asked to be laid to rest here, in a leafy cemetery in Stanmore, observing, in the end, the recommendations of his faith: he hadn't wanted to be sent home. (My mother, too, has chosen to lie next to him when she goes.) Formalities and signatures. (Certificate from doctor and town hall. And questions: what relation are you to the deceased? His one and only son.) We buried him in his chosen place on a Friday. I, his third child, carried him on my shoulder to his grave on a windy December day without rain. His daughters were all there, his first-born who had flown in from in Delhi and the little one from Dhaka, and the middle one, the family's other writer, who lives a few miles away in London (she was the only one of us to see him go, though he was already beyond words). And his granddaughters came with his favourite grandson, breaking the taboo that prevents the presence of women at funerals. And there were others, of other faiths and countries, young and old. He was mourned by many, and the telephone lines rang and rang with missives from the land he had loved so much, erasing all the borders that partitions had drawn. Messages came, and continue to come, from the friends I have made, through my writing, in his native city. They regret the passing of an age and the stories which will never now be told. But I stammer at his death, as I stammered while he lived, and for two months I thought I wouldn't write again. On the first day of January my sisters and their daughters planted flowers on his grave. I wasn't there. On the fortieth day after his death, which fell in the holy month of Ramadan, several generations of friends gathered with us to say words of prayer and goodbye before they broke the day's fast. The fiftieth anniversary of his wedding fell a week or so later, in February. I stayed, unable to look at his grave, with my mother, and turned the pages of the diary of her singing years, which still smells of that garden of frangipani and jasmine I'd so recently seen, the dreamscape of so many of my stories. My ten year old niece Samira, whose father is from England, came home to tell me that the flowers they'd planted in winter – hyacinth, crocus, daffodils – were already in bloom, and the resting-place he'd chosen under foreign skies was very lush and green.

The Fourth Sky
Our Ancestors

At this point I am put in mind to a verse from the Quran which describes those who have lost their way: while there is yet some light they press on a little way; but when the light fails, they again wander aimlessly in the darkness.

Intizar Husain

In the stillness of the night only the footsteps of death were audible – inscrutable death which suddenly appeared and accosted us. But we will bypass it and move on, laughing. Listen! We have complete faith and the conviction born of that love which some even call treason. This treason is nothing but a longing for the fragrance of jasmine blossoms.

Qurratulain Hyder

From THE ALHAQ Sukkur, Saturday 24 October 1914

A SHIKARPUR ROMANCE:
A Buried Page of the History of Mian Mahomed Hoosain [sic] Revived

When the first Nizam-ul-Mulk of Hyderabad, Deccan, died in 1748 AD he left behind him six sons, namely, Ghaziuddin, Nasir Jang, Salabat Jang, Nizam Ali, Basalat Jang and Mughal Ali. He was succeeded in the goverment of the Deccan by the second Mir Ahmad, surnamed Nasir Jang, who was present in Burhanpur when his father died. The eldest, Ghaziuddin Khan, was then residing at Delhi in the office of Amir-ul-Umra [Prince of Princes]. Some years after the death of his father, when his brother Nasir who had succeeded to the throne of the Deccan was assassinated, Ghaziuddin proceeded from Delhi to regain his possessions in that country, but died on on his way at Aurangabad on the 16th of

October 1752 AD. After his death the office of Amir-ul-umra was conferred on his son Shahabuddin with the title of Imad-ul-Mulk Ghaziuddin Khan, by the Emperor Ahmed Shah of Delhi. This is that Ghaziuddin who afterwards became Wazir, imprisoned and blinded Ahmed Shah and assassinated Alamgir II. On account of this his power became weak. He received a jagir [land grant] in Malwa. Subsequently he left and lived in Surat under the protection of the British. Thence he went on a pilgrimage to Mecca. While he was at Surat, he sent his son Mir Bahawuddin Khan to the Kalhora rulers of Sind. He was received by them with great respect; and he arranged to obtain facilities for the British from them in Sind because his father was under British protection. When his father went to Mecca, he decided to take up residence in Sind. Mian Sarfraz Khan, the Kalhora ruler of Sind, granted him the jagir of Kandiaro. During his stay in Sind, Bahawuddin maintained his old friendship for the British, and whenever any opportunity presented itself he obtained concessions for the British Government from the Talpurs who succeeded the Kalhoras as rulers of Sind. When Mir Rustom Khan became ruler of middle Sind, he determined to uproot the family. But Bahawuddin was too powerful for him, and during his lifetime the Talpurs could not summon sufficient courage to oppose him. At last Bahawuddin died at Mithankote as he was going to meet the ruler of the Punjab. He left behind him three sons, Noor Mahomed [sic], Nasurullah [sic] and Mahomed [sic] Yaqub. The eldest was only fifteen at the time of his father's death, and there was no other powerful man in the family.

Mir Rustom Khan of Khairpur, who already had a grudge against this house [though he was, according to my father's papers, a close relative by marriage], took this opportunity to bring about the ruin of it. Having taken their trusted servants in league he plundered all their property and drove away the young boys. Of these treacherous servants Duran Khan Turk and Abdullah Arab went and lived under the Mirs of Hyderabad and died a disgraceful [why, I wonder?] death in the battle of Miani. The three young sons of Bahawuddin lived for some time with the ruler of Multan. At last they migrated to Shikarpur, Sind, because they were disciples of the Sirhindi pirs [sages] who lived there. During those days there lived in Shikarpur one Allahbux, a dyer, who originally belonged to Rohri and was a disciple of this family. With the downfall of the family, he devoted his attention to the service of the young boys. Being in very poor circumstances the boys used to work as labourers. At last they themselves adopted Allahbux's profession of dyeing clothes.

Nasurullah and Yaqub died in the prime of their lives. The eldest brother, Noor Mahomed, lived to a great old age. He left behind him only one son, Mian Mahomed Hoosain, who rose to be an eminent personage and well-known advocate and died in 1900 and left four sons. Mr Ali Buksh is presently Municipal Councillor, Mr Nabi Buksh [whose Afghan wife gave birth to his firstborn son, my father Ahmed, in 1919] is Deputy Collector, Nara Valley, Mr Abdul Kadir is Resident Magistrate, Mehar, and Mr Rasul Buksh is a student in Shikarpur High School.

Sind Gazette

King-Emperor and the Troops From India

The following gracious message from His Majesty the King Emperor to the British and Indian troops arriving in Europe from India, is published for general information:

Message to British Troops

Officers, non-commissioned officers and men, you have been recalled from service in India, together with your comrades from that country, to fight for the honour and the safety of my Empire.

Belium [sic], whose country we are pledged to defend, has been devastated and France has been invaded by the same powerful foe.

I have implicit confidence in you, my soldiers. Duty is your watchword, and I know your duty will be nobly done.

I shall follow your every movement with deepest interest, and mark with eager satisfaction your daily progress; indeed, your welfare will never be absent from my thoughts.

I pray God to bless you and guard you and bring you back victorious.

Message to Indian Troops

Officers, non-commissioned officers and men, I look to all my soldiers to uphold the izzat of the British Raj against an aggressive and relentless enemy.

I know with what readiness my brave and loyal soldiers are prepared to fulfil this sacred trust on the field of battle shoulder to shoulder with their comrades from all parts of the Empire.

Rest assured that you will always be in my thoughts and prayers.

I bid you go forward to add fresh lustre to the glorious achievements and noble traditions of courage and chivalry of my Indian Army whose honour and fame are in your hands.

Times Eulogy

The Times says that no episode in this extraordinary war is more remarkable or inspiring than the presence of Indian troops on the Continent. France will be equally proud of the men who joyously came to fight on her behalf as well as on ours. It will be our part, when we have settled our affair with Germany, to see to it that as the years pass India takes a more ample place in the councils of the Empire.

Verse

Forward! Forward, gallant band!
Forward, over sea and land
Where, upon a foreign strand
Beckons Death or Victory!

Love and Faith and Duty call:
England's honour summons all
By her side to stand and fall
Makers of her history!
Let your dauntless deeds attest
Nobly, proudly to the West
That within the Eastern breast
Throbs a heart as proud and free.
Forward! Forward, gallant band
Forward, over sea and land
Where, upon a foreign strand
Beckons Death or Victory!

by *Nizamat Jung*

10 January 1999

Dear A:

A transcript of a newspaper cutting (details cited above) I found among the papers my father left me. I think it's a fitting appendix to my story. I haven't changed a word; but I have added some commas, deleted some repeated clauses, and the parenthesized notes are, of course, mine. So you see how my Sindhi ancestors, too, were descended from an outsider, and became a local clan that made its name and place and rose and fell and rose again. (I couldn't resist including the contents of the rest of the page. Or cutting out some of the poem's most florid lines.) Bad news and bombs fell on our worlds last year: I'm glad '98 is over. The weather is clement this winter and the days grow longer. Was it Nabokov who wrote that an artist ceases, at some point, to need his fatherland? I've suspended my dreams of return. But the old mother tongue still maintains its hold. In these last days before the onslaught of lessons and deadlines, I make my home in a book of those old legends we knew so well as children. Do you remember the one about the voyager to the Land of Darkness who meets a woman who asks him to pay to watch her piss in the middle of the road and a one-eyed man who demands his sight for staring at him? Where is the land of darkness, then – here or there? I've ceased to wonder. Sometimes I think I live between streets and stories. I walk in the narrow hidden lanes of Marylebone, reddish and cobbled, for hours and think of you all. Memories, like shards of glass, lie shining at my feet in the setting sun. And, like glass, draw blood. Then I taste the rain and the salt and the blue distance and I think of the skies of home.

Give my love to the sea.

A.

Birdcries

For Safinaz

If you watch them long enough, layer upon layer of silver upon silver, forming pictures against the blue-purple: there's an archer, here his bow, three fishes, a throne, a bear, seven princesses, a ram. If you watch them long enough you can hold off tomorrow, tell yourself again there isn't going to be a tomorrow, only these hours without sleep, in which you can find yourself in every constellation, lose yourself in every story the stars tell you.

Fourteen years she's lived and the stars will form the same patterns every night on the same day of the year, whether she wakes or sleeps, stays in the world or not. One hour more, and this Tuesday will be over: her birthday, uncelebrated, unsung. Back again to another dull morning, lost in these backwaters, spring approaching, never quite here, departure delayed day after day. Bright lights beckon from the city where Sameer is, like these stars shooting out their silver petals from the sky, like the flowers shooting out their golden petals from the green all around.

It's still bright enough; the gaslights all along the lane are flickering yellow, trickling out to join the spring lamps in the sky. If she really wants to, Huma can read; *Valley of the Dolls* is under her pillow, concealed in the dustjacket of an ancient mouldy edition of *Anna Karenina*. Across the street, Ravi's begun his nocturnes on the mouth organ, scattering his raw, red notes, doleful at the start, then its pitch rises, and the rythm of the music accelerates.

If Sameer had been here, he'd have whistled plaintively in response; they'd have duetted for as long as it took one of the elders to tell him that at midnight, in this city, decent folk sleep. Sameer would have laughed his running water laugh, then winked at her and burrowed into his patchwork, whispering to her from time to time. But Sameer's gone: tonight he'll be on his way to London, leaving her in this dump, surrounded by old women and dying birds, little difference. And Ravi howls all night long like a wild dog in his garden, with no one to stop him, no one to tie him down.

Huma has had her ears pierced this morning. Sameer left her garnet earrings as a birthday present. When she sees him in London her ears will have healed, and she can change her hoops for the garnets. He'll smile at her again, and tell her she's prettier than her favourite movie star. But she doesn't know when they're leaving.

No use. She can't sleep. She creeps out of bed and tiptoes to the ledge, gravel hissing under her bare soles. She throws her head back in the light breeze, bathes her shoulders in its coolness, lets her long hair whip around her. She looks at the shadows and the stones, whiteness of walls, stars like fireworks. The old moon, a beggar hag with a shawl, white and wrinkled, hides her face in a darkening sky. Around the house lie the dark grounds, the courtyards and the backyards. A childhood companion had been exiled there by her parents, house-servants, last year: pregnant, she'd refused to name the father, and given birth to a dirty, snivelling daughter. Now she wanders around, half-crazy, coughing and coughing; her pink prettiness is yellowing and greying, and she's only nineteen. They say she'll be dead soon, of tuberculosis.

There are other stories, too, of cousins and uncles and beautiful step-sisters, that she always associates with this house. A generation ago a young uncle, who'd become a famous poet at twenty, had developed consumption too, after being jilted by a childhood sweetheart for a richer beau. Another pair, best friends, had duelled over the cousin they both loved, swearing to fight until both fell dead; but one survived, and married the girl who'd loved the other all the time. All these dead stories come alive for her when she lies awake at night; they light up the garden. Even in that distant decade, degrees of cousinhood allowed a wide range of love-matches and meetings: at least they were all your own. It's stepping outside the circle that breaks open their golden ring of fading privilege.

Beneath the balcony where she stands is the front garden, that lies like a boat in the vast sea of the house's grounds. It's a patch of grass, hemmed in by hedges covered in wild berries, and tiny flowers that grow in nosegays of yellow and pink. A few smaller trees grow among the bushes that form the hedge, trees easy to climb though once, as a small child, she was stranded on one of them; she'd been too small to jump off, on Uncle Zafar's shoulder, and he'd had to bring a ladder up to the tree for her to climb down. It's a tiny enclosure, the garden, reached through the front porch by walking past the ancient Bentley that's been there for years and still, sporadically, runs. You pass through the small revolving gate in the hedge and you're in a world of green, sheltered from eyes, a tiny walled city like the grandmother's house, with its rules, its laws, its hierarchies and revered orders.

All around the house and the garden lie the grounds in their wider walls, the stone walls. Mango trees rise, tall and haughty with their green and yellow leaves, from yards of dust. There's a well, surrounded by busy chickens and lazy, timid cows. Beyond it there's a tree which must be the world's tallest. Half a mile behind the house, scary, hairy scavenger hogs feast on refuse from the waste-pits. Dark women in multicoloured skirts and veils, wrists heavy with bright glass bangles and ankles laden with bells of light silver carry fruit baskets, chanting high prayers on their way to their gods with offerings, singing on the way to market with their produce. She thinks of them as the guardians of the fruit trees. Others bring baskets of glass bangles; men come to the porch with baskets of pinenuts, peanuts, walnuts. They watch out for the animals. Bulls sometimes go mad here; they gore a child or even a grown man. Sameer told her once that you have to geld them or they go wild. Children laugh, scream, scrabble in the dust with chickens; they're dressed in a gaudy assortment of their parents' castoffs and hand-me-downs from the grandmother's house. Their hair is bleached by the sun's gold, gilded with the earth's dust. Gipsies come in to sing and dance. Sometimes there's a woman with a bear, but more often you get melodramatic monkeys, acting like marionettes from a Punch and Judy show.

At the foot of the tall tree there's a smooth, conical stone. Huma kicked it once and a woman began to scream: she worshipped there every morning, placing garlands of marigolds, jasmine around the stone, as if it were the image of a god. Sameer grabbed her arm and said:

— Huma, Huma, you don't know their ways, we don't know their customs. Ravi came riding in just then through the gateway. He was eighteen now and had been riding a motorbike for a year. He laughed.

— Don't you know what it is? It's a lingam.

— What's a lingam?

— A phallus, stupid, a holy phallus, they pray to it . . .

And she'd thought, weird people, elephant-headed gods, six-armed goddesses, prayers to penises . . .

∾ ❀ ∾

They'd been here nearly three months now, since they left Ooty. Things were getting worse on the borders. You could hear mother counting on her beads the days before they could leave. It had something to do with a new country being made of what had been East Pakistan. All her life, ever since she could remember, there'd been these wars. Six years ago, Daddy had been stuck in Delhi during a war: he swore he'd been given no trouble, but he came back to Karachi bleak and grey and Mother had stopped singing. He'd had to go all the way on a special plane to Lebanon to get away from India. Contacts between the two countries had broken down completely. Policemen wouldn't stop coming to the house to ask him questions. They'd made Mother thin with care before he returned and still they wouldn't stop. Sameer had told them Father had been interned in Delhi as an enemy alien and now, even in the city of his birth, he was being treated that way. That's why Sameer hated both countries with an ugliness that still made her flinch.

A year after that, Father left for England; he was going to set up business there, and ask them to join him. His sister, who was a widow, persuaded Mother to give up their comfortable rented house, with the backgarden she'd tended so carefully, and come to live with her while arrangements for their departure were being made. After all, Mother could do with everything she could save, to take with her to a strange country. But then Mother had bad news: Father had had a stroke, wasn't talking and hardly moving. She struggled on, alone, for nearly a year; she tried to sell her diamonds to a relative, though she never told her children which one, and the relative said, when she asked for the rest of the money she'd been promised, that what she'd given was by way of a loan and the relative hadn't seen any diamonds at all. Father's sister would disappear to the family estates for months and brothers, uncles and cousins would appear, forcing mother to sign away property, telling her father owed them money, that he'd got himself a bad name by being in India during the war and the best thing to do was to sell up and leave. Mother was a glorified housekeeper to their aunt for more than a year; she slept with her three children in one room, and when the time came for the family to pay her for what they'd extorted from her, or what they owed Father, they'd come up with the same excuse again. Mother got so ill – because she went to oversee some work of Father's far, far out in the countryside when she was already sickening – that the doctors were afraid for her life. Things had become just slightly better with India then. So as soon as she was better she spent what she was able to and sent Maryam, Sameer and Huma away, to her parents. She joined them when she could, though she hadn't wanted to leave Karachi till the last minute. They'd passed their holidays with the grandmother and the year in Ooty, where their uncle had a school; the children could study, and people wouldn't ask too many questions. In the South, they were just People from the North, and even their being Muslims didn't make them much more peculiar. But the minute they were Northbound their Mother told them to speak only English on trains, lest their pronounced accents give them away, and say they came from the North.

But now things were very bad again: in Ooty, Sameer had started getting into fights with boys at school over Pakistan, feeling threatened. He wanted to be with his father. Sometimes Mother said she couldn't make him out: whether his new-found patriotism wasn't so a much a yearning for his fatherland as his need for a father. And even Uncle Zafar, so discreet like all mother's people, said it was time to leave; Mother had changed nationality automatically when she married a Pakistani, and they didn't have Indian passports. So they're here in Rewa, waiting for Father to send for them, and there's trouble in radio announcers' voices, thick like coarse grain bread. A new country's being mentioned. Pakistan would be cut in two. It didn't matter. They were going on. And Sameer will leave tonight for London.

Huma looks at her mother's empty bed; Nour is sleeping downstairs, beside the Grandmother. With the mosquito netting thrown back, the white bed looks moribund: she has a vision of disaster impending. Quick, superstitious, she conjures up a picture of her mother as she looks when she lies asleep, book open by her side or on her bare midriff. At forty-one, she's more beautiful then ever, resplendent. On impulse, Huma lays herself down on the bed for a moment, smells Nour's familiar smells, jasmine, freshly washed muslin. She rises, goes back to the empty roof. Maryam, the eldest, lies there alone; sheets cast off, she's abundant and vulnerable, open like a faintly over-ripe fallen fruit to the moonlight, the breeze, the flower smells. Creepers fill the air with an odour as heavy as honey. In the tall tree that looms over the roof from the little front garden, the owl cries. Maryam's long black waves gush around her face and golden shoulders like a waterfall. Her body's golden, a peach, too full of flesh and juice. Her skirts tangle between her parted thighs; she's sucking the tip of her thumb, like a baby. Like one of those pinups in glossy American magazines men hide behind serious books on library shelves.

Sameer's bed is empty; no one's drawn it in, somehow, though he's been gone a week.

Notes of Ravi's harmonica fuse with the honey night-smells still. He's like a lonely wolf, she thinks again, or a soul in limbo, without his spring companion. And when he isn't playing jazz riffs on his harmonica, he turns the radio up and fills the lane with loud Bombay music. The neighbours don't mind. Not so far away, there's a cinema showing old films; on clear nights, you can hear syrupy dialogues weigh down the air like a political broadcast. From time to time Ravi will play a Kashmiri folksong. Ripples of major-minor, major-minor stir the brook of the melodies. Tomorrow, or the day after, Ravi's parents will be back from their hill-station holiday; a leash around his neck, the stray dog will be kennelled again.

When Huma and the others first arrived here, and the mourning period for the Grandfather was over, Sameer would turn up the sound on the radio, saying: Let's have a party. They'd tune over to a channel playing rock and they'd all dance till late. Nour, just a breath away, would smile in indulgence, leave them to it. Passers-by would stare up from the lane, looking at these strange people, their strange actions, these city people: birds in the night, covered in exotic plumage, trilling strange mysterious bird-cries out into the night.

Ravi at the gate across the lane, sending echoes from his harmonica; Maryam smiling, Sameer waving, you can see that though they can't see him Ravi's smiling too. It didn't matter that he couldn't come up to join them, the rules of the house forbid that; his music, his laughter, were with them.

Then someone complained; or perhaps Aunt Ayesha had seen them indulge in 'foreign frolic'. They were told to turn their music down, not to dance in full view of passing strangers. This wasn't a circus. So they took to singing instead: voices were anonymous, singing a normal part of life even here in Rewa. They'd sing old poems, folksongs, songs from films, Sameer's tenor caressing Huma's flute, pillowing Maryam's wavering contralto. Then Nour, coming out into the freshness in her nightdress with her hair loosened over one shoulder, would join them, her low, clear tones ringing out into the night, shattering the darkness into fine fragments of crystal, into snowy showers of jasmine petals, into sprays of silver light all around them.

Ham to re babul bele ki kalyan
ghar ghar banti jaen re
Ham to re babul
angna ki chiriyan
sanj bhayi ur jaen
Lakhi babul more
Kahe ko byahi bides

Then Sameer took to loping off with Ravi every evening; to the cinema, to his house, to his school or for a drive on his scooter. At first he'd come home at dinnertime, after hanging around with Ravi till then; later, he'd appear at table for an hour or so at most, then off he'd shoot again. Nour would say: He's a boy, he's growing up, he needs other men around him, it isn't good for young men to stay cooped up with women and books. Maryam, nineteen now and lusciously putting on weight with the good bread, dairy foods and fruits of the Grandmother's table, protested one night: But he's always preferred books to people and us to outsiders and then we're not allowed out at all. We may as well be in parda.

— You're ungrateful, Nour retorted, you always have been. We're guests here and haven't anywhere to go until Daddy sends tickets for us from London. In her mother's house, they have to abide by the old rules. They made fun of Ravi – he was good looking, but gauche; spoke terrible English, so that Sameer, too, had grown more used to speaking Hindi; he dressed like a bargain basement Bombay movie star with tight trousers, stiff checked collars, pointed boots and hair smeared with gel. Maryam complained, begged to be sent to Bombay, rancour stitched countless concentric circles into their conversation until Nour was weeping and asking: What do you understand? Life's not an American novel, and Huma thought: Women's lives ARE this way, women wait, women weep, women work, rich or poor, beautiful or ugly, while men sneak off at night to their friends or their whores or their games or their gambling. Women are like birds in the night at their father's homes, caged birds, and melancholy birds singing on snapped branches when left by their husbands at other people's mercy. I don't want it. I'm going to fly away one day.

∾۞∾

One night Uncle Zafar had come upstairs – he was home early from his club that evening for a change, they'd all eaten together and then Nour and the girls had retired and were sitting embroidering sequinned flowers into scarves in the lamplight on the open roof. He called out to Nour, they could hear them talking together softly in English. Maryam and she shared a rare moment of empathy: they'd played his dialogues before in one of their games, they knew his formulations backward. I know I'm the man of the house and should behave like a father to him, but what am I supposed to do for the boy? I'm at college all day ... lessons, tutorials, sports ... and I need some relief, so I play bridge for an hour or two after that ... I know Sameer needs his father but what can I do? He's falling into bad ways with Ravi. Lord knows where they go in town, coming back at all hours, wine and women and song maybe, and then ...

Huma started. Not what she expected. He's talking about cigarettes, THE cigarettes.

— He's not a bad boy, don't misunderstand. Only a little high-spirited. But he's taken to thieving now . . . packs of cigarettes and now . . . two Coronas. Ravi must have put him up to it.

Strange. Nour, inspite of her constant ill-health and her tendency to emotional outbursts, kept completely calm. Very softly, she took up for Ravi first.

— And after all, she went on. A boy who's lived all his life in big cities. The only son of adoring parents. No lack of mental stimulus. Sameer's not asking for much. He's fifteen. He misses his father, misses the freedom he's always had, misses his school, his studies, his companions. Ravi's a good boy and a godsend to him. Then London and plans to get there seem so distant. And I know we're weighing on you now.

— No, no, it isn't that, this is always your home.

— Let me send him to Atiya Apa in Bombay while we're waiting.

And when Sameer crept in later that night, soft up the steps as usual his mother called out to him. Unlike those other times, their tones weren't bantering or playful; they were sombre as a tombstone. Sameer passed Huma's bed; she cowered under her patchwork quilt, guilt melting her entrails like wax, her purloined cigarettes had done this . . .

O Sameer, now you're going, who'll I sing with? I only wanted you back . . .

Sameer walked by, to Maryam's bed. She heard the whispering. What are they doing, trying to wrap me up in cotton wool?

— No, Maryam, don't make a fuss. You stay on with Mama. She's weaker than you think. She takes it out on you. Bear with her, it's only a matter of weeks. It'll be alright. I was leaving for London soon, any way. I was happy enough here, but you know me – I'm happy anywhere I find myself. Bombay, kid. Think of all the movies I'll get to see . . .

— Little bitch got away with it. She's jealous of people breathing.

— Come on, don't blame Huma. She took the fags as a joke and then she panicked. She's always been this way. Don't you remember she bit my ear so hard it bled and then she bawled herself? I got smacked before Mama noticed it was me that was bleeding. That's me and Huma, always has been.

ꙮ❀ꙮ

. . . Leaving her before her birthday – it falls this year on the day of Abbas's martyrdom, when dirges will be sung, not praisesongs – he gives her the garnets, a kiss, and says: See you in Bombay, Humi. Look after Mama and Maryam, you know you can. He tickles her, in the maddening way she loves . . .

Now Huma bites her lip. The memory, and Sameer's departure, still hurt, like a stitch in the side, or an accidentally chewed-upon underlip. Maryam still won't forgive her, Ravi still comes prowling round the courtyard but only rarely now, carrying magazines for Maryam, books for Nour. He asks for Sameer, where is Sameer, is he coming back? No one's told him why he's gone. Traitor. You took him away. If it hadn't been for you.

And that fat, self-righteous cow of a Maryam keeps blaming her silently. But she hasn't given away her secret to Nour. Give her half a chance, though, and she'll tell Ravi what happened; Ravi, who doesn't even smoke. She's just waiting for his widowed mother and his sisters to come home so she'll have an excuse to cross the road to his house or chatter at the gate. He isn't allowed to come upstairs; she only gets to speak to him from the balustrade as he stands on the gravelled drive downstairs.

She lights one of her contraband cigarettes. She'll have to throw it far out, into the grounds over the ledge. She can't put the blame on Sameer, this time. She lies down on her string bed, looking up, once again, at the constellations: a bird here, a cross there, a sword, almost like a comet, and a shooting star – or is it Superman?

The light's growing more faint by the moment; perhaps there's a mist, or the dew's thickened the atmosphere. Or it's drizzling lightly, or the night wind's in her eyes. She rises to put out and discard the barely-smoked cigarette. Runs to the ledge, feels the wind on her face and her hair lash her cheeks. She shuts her eyes; she wants to switch off, one by one, the stars that keep her awake and worrying. But unbidden they keep dancing, forming patterns against the blue-purple velvet lining of her eyelids. Whose face is that I see? Is that you, Sameer, in your black bomber jacket and jeans? But you're not alone. There's Ravi behind you – I know his long hands, I hear the harmonica – but why is the green of his eyes so sad? Look up: Listen, listen to the sound of my wings as I glide softly down the Path of Cows. But don't worry, I won't be off for long: I may come back, to take you away. My starry feathers trail behind me like the Daughters of the Bier while my golden fingers scatter fistfuls of constellations, palmfuls of comets.

The Blue Direction

1

Even in January the sea breeze was humid and heavy with salt and the night sky was the mottled colour of an overripe plum. Music travelled from the cousin's balcony to the boy's in white-hot waves: electronic chords echoing a demonic chorus.

Lucy in the sssky . . .

The boy had been thinking of Kamalakshi the maths teacher for the last three days, since he arrived in Bombay. She was twenty-one and he wasn't yet fifteen. Before Christmas she told him she'd be leaving to get married and she'd miss him. He was merely worried about his algebra then. But when he saw the cousin here, six foot tall and not even sixteen, he began to miss her. To want to complete the story about her. The night fell thicker and heavier and he felt the strings of the drawn-back screen stroke his face. Maybe this is what love is like, he thought, missing someone when the sea's so close and there's music playing and you have only yourself and a memory. A vision of Kamalakshi on a cloud, dressed in cloudy white with hair loose on her shoulders, floated across the sky.

With diamonds . . .

He wrapped the strings softly round his neck and tugged his body forward. Reached the chair. Sat down. Rocked himself.

— What the fuck . . . (the cousin walked in.) You'll kill yourself.

Just seeing what it's like to die for love, he wanted to say, but the cousin would think he was crazy. So he laughed.

There was a smell of burning flesh on the breeze. Maybe they were burning a dog. Fuad grabbed your arm and said: Come on, come to my room. The first time he'd done that, since you got to Bombay. But then you'd been the one to stay silent, keep to this room, spend your time here. There was something about your long-haired, sweat-stained cousin in his cricket whites, suddenly tall and articulated like a grasshopper, that annoyed you. Not any more, though. He's still a child, with all his music and his drum kit and his girlfriends and his car. A big braggart of a little boy.

2

Time up, too soon: now it's back to the blue mountains. After the fun of movies and music and walks by the sea and talking to cousin Fuad about the maths teacher halfway into the night. Your parents were always leaving behind these cities by the sea, or sending you away, you were used to it by now. Thirteen months ago mother had put you on a plane from Karachi to Bombay and in forty-five minutes you were in this other city where the sea was the same but smelled different and you weren't supposed to say where you came from because there was always trouble on the borders and in this climate you were enemy aliens. Six months ago you'd driven across the country in the heat with your father and the car that carried you broke down in a fly-infested dungheap of a southern village where you spent half a day with your face covered by a handkerchief soaked in cologne to keep off the sun and the insects. Sweat still poured down your temples into your ears. You drove through cities where you stopped for a night or so and you read about Oscar Wilde and Sarah Bernhardt in dusty old libraries no one had used since the Raj dusted off its crimson bottom and rode away on its lame nag. A night or so in an air-conditioned room was worth the odd spat with your father whose comforting ruddy plumpness concealed taut, lightning-voltage nerves. Which you, when no one else was there, seemed quick to ignite. The landscape changed after Coimbatore: another country, of palms and bare-breasted women carrying baskets on their heads. Flavours matched colours, sour giving way to sweet and everything inflammable and reeking of coconut. At Mettupalayam the car began the ascent, past two jungle reserves where you could see clumsy dowager elephants waddle by, up a sequence of nauseous hairpin bends flanked by eucalyptus trees that housed little bands of monkeys busily picking lice from each other's pelts, through a town or two of dizzying anonymity, to your destination. When you turned the window down to stanch your sickness a blast of cold air slapped your face in spite of the sunlight and May. You drove through a dense grove of ferns and other foliage past the faint suggestion of leafy water to the red-gabled villa that stood in the shadow of camellia and magnolia trees – textures of red and white and a sweet, faintly venomous smell equally unfamiliar – on top of a low hill. Behind the house were the stables which looked little villas too: your father had come here to breed and house horses and provide studs for race-horse owners. He'd been a fine polo-player in his youth. You ran down to the lake as soon as you'd put down your suitcase in the big double room your father said was going to be yours.

This time, though, they'd gone to pick up the mother. She was coming back from Karachi, still thin and ravaged by the sickness that had felled her two years before. And this time it's the mother who takes him back. By train. The journey lasts three days. The trains lurch, spewing out their fumes like stunted dragons, through that unbearable alien landscape of palms. The little toy train takes them to the town where they live, the blue mountains' highest town. They take a taxi to the red-gabled villa which the boy, with a tense awareness of clichés, still can't abide to call home. (Home was once in another country. A house on a hill, where the mother grew maize and watermelons and nurtured orchids with ordure and bits of broken glass, and the boy read Hans Christian Andersen and tales of Greek heroes and Arabian knights all Sunday long in the almond tree's shade, and the rain fell only a few days in summer with a low cry like a peacock's, and the earth smelt like crushed jasmine before the rain fell, like split papaya while it was falling and, after the storm, like a potter's kiln. They left that home nearly two years ago.) You don't call a place home more than twice, he knows that now. And he knows they haven't made a home in this country, either, not yet, that's why they're lying low, like fugitives, in this strange little town which doesn't care too much about passports and papers and doesn't call you enemy aliens. This mountain town which, with its foreign street names and its houses that belong to another era, reminds him of one of the urban scenes enclosed in those glass paperweights Dad used to bring back from his travels. Except that something's wrong here, the dark faces and the metallic speech and the virulence of the green verdure don't match the demure houses. Beyond the flower shows and the dog shows and the horse races and the boat races, beyond the forced gaiety of the tourist season, there's something else.

There are the women who clean homes during the Season and work in the potato fields when the tourists go away. Four of them came to work in the villa on trial when they first arrived and the mother took to the smallest, darkest one, because she sang while she cleaned in a low, rasping voice full of lilting nuances like a gipsy's violin. Her name was Rehmat. The tall, fair one who seemed to have taken charge muttered:

— You know what she does when the foreigners go away? She stands at the corner of the market, by the cinema, and it's not flowers she's selling, the only flowers she's got are in her hair. If you know what I mean. Her husband left in his truck when her second son, who's twelve now, was born. Never comes back. And her youngest girl's just three. I said what I said, Ma. Don't make me say more.

— You needn't, the mother said. Necessity makes us do all sorts of things. All the more reason to keep her.

She did. And dismissed the others that evening.

There are those who have stayed on because – when India declared itself free – they tried to go back and found that Home had become a foreign place. Children or in-laws didn't want them. Prices in England were high and post-war food disgusting. And – after all – they'd given this country their lives. No one bothered them here and the mountain air was kind enough to their paleness and the rain brought back the shires and counties they'd never see again. So they grow old in the blue mountains, the Turners and the Carters and the Coopers and the Taylor-Moores, making cheeses and arranging dahlias in vases, roasting lamb (or buffalo meat) on Sundays, walking their dogs and borrowing novels by Kingsley Amis and Muriel Spark from the crumbling library with its shelves that house covens of moths, fighting over three-month-old issues of Queen and occasionally mourning their dead. Waiting, for a message or a parcel or – Jesus willing! – a visit from a daughter or a son or a nephew.

There are the high-cheeked bronzed Tibetans in the market and braided tribal elders clad in togas and, even in this tiny place, beggars without hands and feet wheeling themselves in carts with cries of hunger when they see food cast away by passersby who've eaten enough. The boy has seen them eat: Icecreams licked and discarded by fat tourist children and he's wondered what ice tastes like inside a hollow belly on a chill May day. Raw chillies and chicken's feet. Dead chameleons slung on bare black backs. He suffers when he doesn't have a coin to give to them, though he knows that his coins aren't enough to take away even one person's hunger.

There are the teachers at the school: two or three callow young men from the plains who are obviously on their way to better things if this place doesn't trap them forever in its cricket fields and its chemistry labs. Parents waiting for money-orders, sisters waiting for dowries. The Annadurais and the Appadurais, folding away in camphorated trunks their dreams of bright lights and big cities. Two or three blooming young women seeing young brothers through school, or saving for their own dowries. If time allows. (Look at her, she got away at twenty-one, but then she's fair like a swan and we're dark like crows, says Beth the chemistry teacher about Kamalakshi the maths teacher.) If time allows. (And what will time allow to the others, the widows and the divorcees, hiding here from the monsoons and the duststorms of the plains, far from their own sons? Backrooms in the homes of their daughters-in-law when they reach sixty and give way, backs bent and eyes squinting with chalk dust, to the new gaggle of callow maidens and youths who stop by on their way to marriages or bright lights or even a voyage across the black waters?)

(And what will you be, you wonder, when you are older – and the sun is setting in the lake and the ferns whisper, Hurry home, but you dawdle – will you draw pictures or will you sing songs – and the clock in the old churchyard strikes six and the graves say hurry home and your footsteps are quicker on the path up the steep hill – or write stories, will you cross the stage with great galloping steps like the pirate . . . and there's a sickle moon rising pale in the glassy sky but the clouds are still orange-bright . . . Will you leave for a big, bright city? Or will you teach bored boys about the travails of obscure Jude or the history of dead kings in this little town?)

The future's not ours to see, the mother used to sing as she soaped their bottoms.

Whatever will be, will be.

Que sera, sera.

3

The first friends the boy had made in the town were his teachers. Miss Stella Sarkissian, who'd come all the way from Calcutta twenty-two years before, in the year the country was set free, and lived with the Mackinlays in the centre of town. And Sarada Menon, whom the boys all affectionately knew as Saradakka. Her short round body draped in a tidy white sari with muted border, her huge coil of greying hair unravelling itself on the nape of her neck, she'd been born in Calicut on the other side of the mountains but travelled around the country as a civil servant's daughter before (as she put it) the country was carved up, and then spent the fifties and early sixties in Sri Lanka where she'd left behind a drunken husband and two daughters. Sarkissian taught music and drama and painting; Sarada taught English, Hindi and History. The authors they were studying for the school certificate were Shakespeare, Hardy, Eliot and Orwell. (The boy had always preferred Hugo, Sand, Flaubert and Zola – not to mention Mérimée and France – but Sarada has a compelling way with Hardy's Charmonds and Gileses, ripping up padding and upholstery to reveal nuts and bolts of frustration, rejection, desertion and despair which made him thrill. But he loved those other stories, of captains and kings, so drily told in set textbooks, even more: Sarada says he got an A in the history exam because he made something so readable of chronologies and raw facts that it was more romance than chronicle.) The school's rough lads would mock him: Pull down your trousers, show us what a carved-up Muslim cock is like. He'd spit at them. He was bad at sciences: Kamalakshi, who was twenty-one, gave him special tuitions in maths the first term. Sometimes her breath grazed his face as she leaned over to correct his fractions; sometimes her nails grazed his fingers. Once she asked him: Why are you staring at me? He didn't know he was. The first summer Sarkissian invited him to her house for tea and he met the Mackinlays. Sarkissian is tall and thin and on her forays into town she wears a black velvet cap. The Mackinlays are short and stout and grey and look like twin weasels: tousled crops of carrot-grey, freckles the colour of teacakes, shirt-sleeves rolled up to elbows, shapeless tweed trousers. Molly makes cheese for the dairy near the library, Mack breeds fox terriers. On Saturday afternoons they drive him to the library. All through the summer, through the rainy days that follow when the town's drenched in darkness and the wood fires are lit and the beasts howl loud in the rocks at night, Sarkissian tries to make a painter of him, and he wants to capture everything he sees in smudged colours, but he can't stay within the outlines he's sketched. He can draw, though. And act. Sing. Write. By the time the year had ended, before he left for Bombay, he'd been auditioned and cast in the operetta they were going to stage in the town hall in summer, at the peak of the season, to mark the moment when the blue flowers that gave the mountains their name would be in bloom for a very short season. (Blue flowers that, local lore had it, blossomed only once in twelve years.) Sarkissian was composing and designing, Sarada directing. (I played King Lear in Delhi when I was twenty-one, she says.) Boys' parents would have come up by then, to pick up their sons, they'd say, but what they wanted was a chance to escape the heat of the plains and bet a bit on the horses. A grand occasion for all.

4

Late January. Frost glazed the mountain paths, turning soil and stone into treachery. You walked the three miles to school every day, in your baggy pants and your too-tight blazer. You had to use your tall umbrella as a stick when you walked up and down the hills. Rain fell so fine you couldn't escape its freezing talons. You wore a cap and, under your dung-coloured mac, three layers of black wool. Days were grey, smoke-laden. Kamalakshi the maths teacher had left, but there was still the play to keep you busy.

It was taken from an old tale he knew, though the boy couldn't remember who had told it to him; he thought he'd heard it from an old labourer with a red beard who was working on a site opposite his house in Karachi. But Sarkissian said, over tea and hard cheese and scones (made by Molly Mackinlay), that it was an old Armenian legend, and Sarada said it was based on a Punjabi ballad she'd heard when she was studying at Kinnaird College in Lahore. It went like this:

The Captain and the Prince of Persia

In a faraway land long ago, there was a king who was good but too proud. To punish him, a wise man blinded his only daughter and blighted his fertile land. Only the Flower of Love, plucked by the hand of a virtuous person, could redeem him. So the king summoned Aazad Bakht, the captain of his fleet, a man he trusted above all others, and commanded him to find the flower. Aazad travelled the seven seas but no one had heard tell of the miraculous flower. Exhausted, careworn, he stumbled home on the night of the full moon. His garden was alight with lamps and torches were fastened to every tree. His bride, whom he had left behind with her parents a bare two weeks after their nuptials, ran down the marble staircase to greet him, draped in bright garments. Welcome, voyager, she said. Welcome home on the night of the Flower of Love. That was the very flower the King wanted. Falling to his knees, the captain begged his wife's indulgence, asking her to sacrifice to their nation's good, with her own fair fingers, the magical flower. But on the way back to the royal city, Aazad encountered an old man with a racking cough. What ails you, friend, asked the valiant captain. I have been searching, fine sir, for the Flower of Love to bring back the light to my blind daughter's eyes and the dark, dark roses to my rose garden. So familiar a story! The captain's kind heart began to melt, and he yearned to give the flower from his cloak to the old man, but his duty to sovereign and nation forbade him. He said his farewells after giving the old man the remaining portion of bread and fruit he had carried from home, and set off. Exhausted, he lay down to sleep ten miles from the gate of the city. While he slept, the old man dealt him a mighty blow on the head and stole his flower, and threw off his skilful disguise, revealing himself as a handsome man of wealth and fortune. When Aazad arose, with his skull bleeding, the flower was gone. He returned to the court, stopping on the way at the clinic of an apothecary who bandaged the gallant captain's head, wondering all the way what would be worse: To confess his guilt to his liege, or admit he had failed in his mission? Chastened, the brave but unwise captain presented himself at court. Wait, he was told, the King is welcoming his distant kinsman, the young Prince of Persia. And Aazad was shocked to see the Prince present the treasured blossom to the King! He pushed his way through the crowd, his customary deference forgotten. So you are the rogue who stole this from me! he shouted. The King, for love of his captain, told him to tell his tale. Which he did. But the wily Prince, who had come to claim the bride who would bring to him the crown and the throne of this rich land, said: This evil man, whom I met on the road and befriended, accosted me and tried to take my life to steal from me this blossom with its magical properties. He wants nothing less than your throne and your daughter's hand! The King ordered the gallant captain's arrest, and on the day of his beheading, which the entire city's inhabitants turned up to witness, the captain was asked if he had one, last request. The captain asked that his body be divided in five parts: one for his men and one for the sea, one for the motherland and one for his mother: but the fifth part, his heart, should go to his beloved, to replace the blossom she had nurtured and so foolishly sacrificed to a vain king's whim. And where this proud, true heart was planted, a hundred magical blooms should grow, as salve for the wounds of the blind and the needy.

❧ ✿ ❧

— Sometimes I think we should give it a happy ending, Sarkissian says. Have the prince confess his misdeed to the princess bride who then begs for amnesty, or better still have the captain's wife tear off her veil and tell the truth. But we have only seventy-five minutes in which to tell our tale and sing our songs. Jai, of course, will be captain Aazad Bakht. And you will play – Sarkissian's twitter rises to the nests and the treetops – The Prince of Persia!

Disappointment silences the boy. But Sarkissian hasn't noticed his chagrin. Or if she has, she's covering it up.

— Of course, Jai will play Aazad, she says. He's tall – and he sings so loudly. Fearlessly. You know, if I hadn't heard him and the others massacre that already ghastly song at the Christmas do, I'd never have thought of it! You nearly got the part, you know? But, dear, you're still growing and your voice is true, but it's small. You couldn't really handle those big sea numbers. And then Sarada pointed out that the Prince needed . . . Well, what you've got, you know? Subtlety. Style. That Jai . . . he's like a pirate!

You should be pleased that she thinks you've got style. No one has told you that before. But you wonder what it takes to gain Jai's courage. His ease and confidence. It was Christmas. You remember it well. Teachers and students sang sugary hymns and theme songs from movies: Somewhere my love, This is my song, I must have done something good. Then the lights went out and you can swear there was smoke in the room. A fiendish role of drums and then the singing began. Behind a screen. A high voice, reedy but strong, with a lower echo booming somewhere and an upper break like a flute changing registers. You could see his profile silhouetted on the screen. Curly, wild hair – longer than the regulations of the school allow, but then it's nearly holidays – hawk nose and long, long hands casting huge shadows on the canvas blankness. They were singing Lucy in the Sky with Diamonds. That bloody song your cousin played all January. You found the performance embarrassing and yet . . . your scorn is inflected with envy.

Jai belonged to an informal gang called the Devil's Stones. He wasn't, though he looked like one, the leader – that honour belonged to his inseparable companion, short, tough Mani, who was taught History by Saradakka along with the boy. Mani frightened him.

One February day, after class, Mani followed him to the fern tree below which he ate his cheese sandwiches (though he has friends now, he still prefers to eat alone and spends most of his recesses in the school's tiny library). Pretended he wanted to look at the boy's notes. Sat too close to him, knocked his knee-bone against the boy's. The boy thought of Heathcliff when he looked at Mani's thick lips and white wolf teeth and fleshy thighs. Knew Mani wasn't interested in the notes at all.

— Shucks, put those away, man. Relax. Cool it. You're a day boy, yes?

— Yes.

— Ever go to the movies? (His arm around the boy's thin back).

— Sometimes.

— Jayalalitha flicks?

— Don't understand two words of Tamil.

— Hollywood movies?

— Usually . . .

— Seen the Chink woman?

— Which one? (Of course you have. From the Golden Bowl, between the library and the bookstore. With her fat floury face and her frizzy dyed hair and her waddling walk with a tie-and-dye skirt slipping down her hips. And yes, you've seen Mani with her but you're not going to tell him that. The pig.)

— You know the one I mean. (His fingers had slipped into the boy's jersey, above his nipple, pinching the fine skin through the cotton shirt, his rough affection no longer a game: this was minatory.) The prossy. Takes us to her room above the cinema and gives us beer and lies down flat on her back and spreads her legs. Ohhh, she's got a pussy like a whale's. (A rude outward gesture with both his arms.) Took two of us at once while the other two watched. Well, not that wimp of a Jai, he walked out. Sat and drank a beer outside.

(You know what those boys get up to in town; or you can guess. You've seen them there. You'd thought Jai too snooty to join them. But he's probably bored.)

— You know whose pussy Jai's into, don't you? Ever asked yourself why your favourite teacher got sent away?

The boy grabbed Mani's hand and pushed him off. The sun hung white in the mid-March sky. The light was like lukewarm water. In the distance lay the lake, a leafy mirror in the shade of the breeze-ruffled fern and eucalyptus. A huge yellow dahlia bloomed alone a foot away from them.

— That hurts.

— Oh, little flower, I never guessed you had such power in those tiny muscles, but I'd never hurt you, now would I? But I know you've seen me in town. You wouldn't tell on me? No? Little virgin? Aren't you a virgin? Tell you what. Come home with me to the Palghat estate this summer and I'll get you a nice village girl with a pussy as tight as this. (He squeezes his fist.) Only five rupees. I'll have her first, of course. I'll teach you. You can watch. Would you like that, little virgin?

The boy sat still, felt Mani's hot repellent chewing gum breath on his face, was transfixed, like a frog hypnotized by the crystal in a snake's eye. Sudden, like a whip, Mani rose slightly, turned so he was facing the boy, pushed his knee between the boy's legs so he felt the weight of his heavy thighs, saw his great brown buffalo eyes and the grains of his dark eyelids magnified. Before he had time to move away, Mani's moist mouth sucked his upper lip. He wiped off the spittle as Mani, laughing with his head thrown back, swung away on the balls of his feet and ran, like an urchin, up the hill to the playing field, looking back only once to call out:

— Don't forget now, will you, little flower, my place at Palghat, this summer?

He bent over, index finger tapping a lip, widened his eyes, then turned, pace reduced to a jog.

Mani avoided him for the next few days, but the boy still felt stalked. Jai was there at rehearsals. Watching him, his almond eyes dark below his curly fringe. Satan's emissary. Doing Mani's bidding.

— I believe this belongs to you, Sarada said to Mani. I didn't know you took such an interest in Hindi.

It was a paper pellet Mani had been sneakily trying to slide over the table to the boy.

— But wait. Let's see what we have here. *Ham tum se pyar karta hai.* Oh, no, Mani, drop any idea you may have of switching from Tamil to Hindi. You've used the first-person plural pronoun with a third-person singular verb. And to whom, pray, is this missive of affection addressed, surely not, I take it, to me? Or is it for your class-mate?

She handed it to the boy, who saw his own name written above the words I LOVE YOU scrawled in green ink, the crude large Hindi letters probably learnt by rote. He averted his face and handed over the letter to Mani, whose *café sans lait* skin was turning aubergine.

After the class – he'd succeeded in avoiding Mani's eyes – Sarada held him back.

— What is it, child? You look so scared all the time.

— Nothing, Miss.

— Has that wretched boy been pestering you?

Mani was waiting, but he stayed in step with Sarada and the older boy loped away.

— What is it, child? Your voice is a whisper today, is your throat sore? Sarkissian asked.

It was time to speak to someone.

In March, the Devil's Stones were expelled. That terrible word. Expelled indiscreetly, before the holiday started. Rumour was, the boy would be given the Captain's role, but who'd play the Prince of Persia then?

Now the sun shone every day. In April, you turned fifteen just before the spring term began. You were the tallest boy in the school, with Jai gone. Hair was sprouting under your arms and your white shirts were stained with acrid perspiration. At night you dreamed of Kamalakshi running past lashing waves in soft focus while you lay on a beach alone and watched. Skies for three days at a time were the turquoise colour you remembered from the beaches of your city. All you had to do was look at Kamalakshi – her bare golden midriff, her waving brown hair – and you woke up with a series of shudders, sweat-drenched and pyjamas sodden. Once you dreamed of Kamalakshi riding down the white strand on a black horse with a star on his forehead, riding towards you, but as you ran, in slow motion like the man in the cigarette commercial, ran toward her, Jai emerged from the shadows, strode to her on his stork's legs. Pulled her off the horse. Kissed her.

At first the boy thought he was wetting his bed as he hadn't done since he was two but when he started to strip the sheets every second day or take cold showers in the middle of the night his father sat him down and told him what it was all about. Nocturnal emissions, he called it. Still, the boy felt tainted, soiled, as if, somehow, Mani's hot breath, his clammy hands, were clouding his visions, smudging them, leading him towards grotesque fantasies.

Back to school at the end of the month. To be faced by his nemesis: Jai had returned. Playing the Captain's role. Rehearsals turned into hell. Well, at least it wasn't that rascal Mani. They said Mani had refused a second chance, but Jai, whose uncle paid for his expensive schooling, quietly telegraphed to say he'd be here at the start of term. He was back, aloof and arrogant as ever but quieter, striding about alone without his mates. He must have known that the boy had set the trap Mani had fallen into at the cinema – where they'd approached him for money or cigarettes. Sarkissian, who'd seen it all from her strategic hiding place, had reported the encounter to Sarada. Thence, the headmaster and the powers that be were a footstep away.

The cousins arrived. One from Delhi, the other from Bombay. One in a flurry of packages, the other with a rucksack. Eighteen year old Fawzia and sixteen year old Fuad. Much of the time Fuad, as ever sweaty and tousled, went off on his own, on horseback or on foot. He took his gun and his fishhook to the hills, though there was never evidence of prey or catch. Fawzia – bony, doe-eyed, crop-haired, with her flapping flares and pendulant white op-art plastic earrings and matching shades in emulation of her idols Audrey Hepburn and Sharmila Tagore – followed him around, because he's the only one who knew the paths and the shortcuts over the green hills and the downs, and she played games with the boy. Or he played those games with her he'd learned from literary romances. On the lake, in a boat before the sun went down, he'd bend towards her, close, as he rowed, so she could feel the heat of his eyes. In the garden, he tickled her neck and probed the pale-olive bone between her breasts with a twig of jasmine. One day she seemed to like him, the next she didn't give a damn. A bunch of flowers she'd pestered him to gather for her from some precarious rock would lie crushed and discarded, crumpled petals reminding him, incongruously, of a small dead bird.

She had a boyfriend in Bombay: to keep her away from him, she'd been sent off here on holiday by her mother, who didn't like him because he'd left behind a wife and a daughter in Detroit, Michigan, and he was far too old for Fawzia. The boy knew he wrote letters to her here and she regularly responded. She hid a passport photo of him in her brassiere, which she'd take out and kiss with open lips when the boy was watching. But her passion didn't prohibit dalliances with the boy, whom she'd surprise in his bedroom while he was undressing with demands for a cigarette which he, who had smoked just once in his life when an uncle had dared him to finish his reeking cigarillo, was unlikely to have. She'd be in a transparent chiffon négligée and when the boy looked at her, she'd say: Never seen a woman's boobies before, you dirty little thing? Once she walked into the bathroom, which didn't lock, while he was shaving off four hairs sprouting from his cheeks, and licked his ear. He turned round, mildly desperate by now, and she opened her mouth wide for his kiss, licked the inside of his lips. But when he tried to put one hand on her shoulderblade, holding his father's foam-sodden cutthroat razor in the other, she escaped and ran. That night, she persuaded Fuad to french kiss her in front of the boy, saying: Let's give him a lesson, he doesn't know how to kiss yet, the little thing.

The lake in the evening was the colour of a blood orange. The echoing pathos of some Irish song he'd heard years ago would summon up the flapping wings of swans overhead, white swans leaving the water on their way to the sky. But there were no swans here in the hills. Only the great wounded sun which was too clumsy in its nightly drunken lurch across to resemble any self-respecting bird. Except, perhaps, an owl of brass.

5

— I met your teacher Sarkissian at the market, says Ma. Did you know her friend – Miz Whatzername – is dead? Of a massive stroke, last night, in the library. She'd gone into the smoking room for a drag of her pipe. She'd been dead for an hour, probably, before Ramanujan went in to lock up at seven thirty.

The boy runs down his hill and up hers to see Stella. (They'd been rehearsing together till eight last night; then she'd driven him almost all the way home, dropping him off at the foot of the hill. He'd had his mind on Jai: imagining the older boy was staring at him as they rehearsed, he would turn round, furtive, to see Jai averting his eyes.)

— She's left me her drunken old Mack and her dying old dog to look after, says his friend, her eyes dry but shot with scarlet threads of sleepless rumination – as she pours amber-golden China tea into flowered cups and hands him a coconut macaroon at the same moment, looking more than ever like a black-wigged lady camel in her grim mourning clothes.

— God knows how I'll live without her. How I'll look after him. Well, on with the show: at least I've got our opera to keep me going.

You realize she's speaking aloud as the habitually lonely often do, of a love you only half understand, forbidden, perhaps, but true, all the same, a love that lasted half a lifetime: luminous, a hyacinth reflected in a teardrop, it had brought them in search of its blue fragrance to this god-forgotten eyrie of a town, where the whispers of school boys, the grumblings of an irate spouse, the nudges of onlookers had ceased to permeate the leather winter hides in which they'd learned to wrap themselves, these two women now old, the she-camel and the weasel lady. Then death comes to the weasel lady and pop she goes, Molly Mackinlay's departed: and may her lord Christ rest her soul! And the she-camel's left alone to look through the needle's cataracted eye. Stella Sarkissian lives on. Plays Chopin in the dark hours. Stands by deaf old Mack's side at the grave.

— God gives us strength to bear our losses, says Ma, pulling her dark shawl to her temples over her dark vital hair.

— I wish I could believe in Him, says Stella. Like Mack does. He's sure she's resting in His bosom.

Mrs Mack's fox terrier Pluto lies down on his mat and dies the morning of the funeral service. They lay him with her in her grave.

You remember the prayer Ma once read out from one of her dear friend Annie Q's Urdu stories:

Hail Mary, Star of the Sea, Sister of the Rocks, teach us to sit still.

6

There was a curdled mist even in the early afternoon, but the seniors and pre-seniors massed around the old well after lunch, trying to chase away the settled frost from their bones with a dose of absent sunlight. The boy sat on the ledge of the well, eating his cheese sandwich, with *The Woodlanders*, on which Sarada would pontificate this afternoon, flopping greenly open on a knee. The scent of eucalyptus made him, as usual, sneeze. At the edges of his vision, he could sense Jai looking over the fence at the twisted lane that led down the town's centre, where he'd cavorted only short months ago. For once, the stork-legged presence of the older boy left him no feelings of anxiety or guilt. The watery light stroked the ferns, which looked a green darker than ever after the morning's shower. Jai turned, tentative, then walked over, as if in a trance, to the side of the well closest to the wall of the lab, just where the boy was sitting. He scrambled up the ledge with his head still turned away toward the lane or the leaves, and sat down. Without knowing how or why, the boy looked up from *The Woodlanders*, which he'd raised before him as a shield, and looked into Jai's eyes.

— Hi. Boring bloody Hardy today, ahn?

— I like him. Here. Have an apple. Rehearsal s'afternoon, right?.

— Yeah. Two-thirty. Thanks, I love apples. Never enough fruit here. Let's go up to the playing field and run over our lines, shall we? We've got half an hour.

7

So simple. He must want to get at you for what you did, chasing away his mates. So you don't know why you've agreed to go up the hill with him. But you're wrong. Halfway through your corny dialogues – (everything's about betrayal, the prince and the captain, traitor and victim) – you change your lines. Try to tell him something about your role in his banishment. But it isn't important. Then you're telling him about Fawzia, about girls and kissing. You're already friends. You didn't know you'd wanted friends, wanted one friend, but now it seems as if you only ever wanted this, nothing else.

— Look, that thing about ratting on the Devil's Stones to Sarada. It doesn't matter. You didn't even know me. Sarada and Sarkissian used you to get at the gang and at me. I was only half-way a member. You must have heard about me and Kamalakshi. It wasn't my fault. I'll tell you another time. She's Sarada's niece, did you know? And the other guys, they were out of line. Then that moronic fink of a Mani had a thing about you. I didn't know soon enough or I'd've told him to lay off. Listen, I've got to study, got to work, my uncle's paying for me, I count as a foreign student. I need a friend here, now. I've had girlfriends, many, and I've liked one or two. But never a guy who I could trust as a friend. Not even that silly arse of a Mani. He let me down, in the end, we weren't even speaking. I like you. I really do. But don't cheat on me now that we're friends, that I couldn't take.

Jai held out both his hands to the boy.

T. Jaisurya Nair. Curly hair, big toothy grin, tall as a man at seventeen, stands nearly six, two inches taller than you but you're daily growing. He was raised in Hongkong, studies sciences. Plays piano, wants to be a musician, but that's probably unlikely. Came here a year before you did, so he's a stranger too, with a foreigner's passport, perhaps, like yours, but not an enemy alien, his people are Nairs from Kerala, and his uncle lives in Travancore. You, too, had another place once. A city by the sea. A white and coral house on top of a hill with a great garden. You weren't allowed to talk about that before you met him. But you can tell him about it, not all of it but about the good times, those, at least, and leave out the rest, stay with the good times, the jasmine and the hibiscus and the white sand and the light hot drops of rain, they're enough, forget about the passport concealed in the drawer, the bad times don't matter any more.

— Do you know, he says to you, sitting on the hill above the playing field in the fern's shadow with the light turning his brown eyes into liquid amber, do you know what it's like to imagine someone, a friend you've always felt at your side, you even know his shape and size but until you meet him you didn't even know you knew or what you knew? I don't want to be soppy. But. You're like that for me.

You know, you understand. But you don't need to say much. You don't need to say anything. So you talk to him about the sea or the air raid shelter you hid in from the Indian shelling in '65 or your trip to Pompeii the same year (where you saw forms frozen into stones of death). And he tells you about flying to Taiwan and Singapore where you too want to go one day, or he chants the names of outlying islands – Wanchao, Nikuchao – in dipping Cantonese that make you fall about guffawing.

You remember a story your mother made you read to her under the almond tree when you were eleven (to practice your slow Urdu recitation) about a man who all his life recalls the blue lake he played beside as a boy, all his life remembers the lake's blue waters and that's enough. You, too, had a blue lake then, not a mile away from your gate. But it's not blue water or yourself as a boy you remember: it's the sea you yearn for, the sea on which your friend and you are sailing in your wanderings, it's always there, a promise, waiting for you, the tight bright blue diamond-studded tarpaulin of sky that shelters you both this May touches that sea, is touching it right now, in Bombay, Karachi, Hongkong, the sea is waiting, calling, calling you both, tomorrow is the sea.

Where there's blue there has to be a sea.

Tomorrow and a sea.

You were born in April. Two years to the day before me.
Since we met I don't need any friends. No one else.
I know. Me neither.
Which one of us is talking?
No, not talking. Singing.

Walking with Jai to the well. The sun's out today.

— On Saturday I took Fawzi to the boats, as usual . . . she said I'd been ignoring her. A man was waiting for her when we came ashore. She introduced him to me as Vinod. He said he'd buy us a coffee at the club, and when Fawzi begged me to go I said yes, it wasn't too late and I really had been ignoring her and Fuad has no time for her any way. We went to the club and after an hour or so of coffee and silly talk Fawzi told me to go home and when I said what'm I to tell Ma, then, she said say what you like, I'm staying here with him. I took a taxi back and made the driver wait while I told Daddy and Ma. Daddy went off with Fuad, took the police to the club where they found her in some sort of bad state, they're not saying, she came home and Ma took her to her room and she's not allowed to talk to me, her Mum's arriving to take her back to Delhi, she won't talk to me so I'm in the doghouse with everyone, her because I told them where she was, and them because they think I was in on Vinod's coming and still begged them to let me take her alone to the boathouse. Fuad's the hero of the whole show this time because it seems he was on to them. And the worse thing is, Fawzi told me it's Vinod's being a Hindu that her mother minds most.

— I'm a Hindu too, of sorts. Never thought much about it really. I eat beef and all. But listen. Kamalakshi used to call me to her room at night for private tuition, she said. One night she started crying and saying: They're marrying me off to a Nair and you know what Nair men are like. (I am one, I suppose, but I don't know what the rest are like, not really.) Anyway. She put her head on my shoulder, and she was so little and pretty I hugged her. Lots of things happened then and after. But one evening she wanted take her things off and . . . you know, go all the way . . . I just couldn't. I don't know who said what to who but you know she's Saradakka's niece and the long and the short of it was she was sent home. I know you . . .

— Yeah, I liked her too. You know. Funny, somehow, I suppose I should be jealous but . . .

— Jealous of who?

— You of course. I told you I really thought I liked . . .

— But you and me, we're different. Since I met you . . .

. . . *I don't need* . . .

. . . *Sometimes we say the same words at the same time.*

. . . *Which one of us is talking now?*

. . . *Singing, I said.*

8

— They're on to you, you know, said Sarada, pushing her recalcitrant spectacles up the high bridge of her nose.

— Me? On to me? About what? They always knew I had a Pakistani passport.

— No. Not that. It's about you and that ghastly Nair boy. They're talking about you. Your partnership is making you conspicuous. They say you're furtive. Conspiratorial. Gardeners don't like weeds. Or wildflowers. It's too sudden, too soon after the expulsion scandal, and he's older. He's as bad as that mate of his, Mani, difficult to say who spoilt whom. Keep well away from him, I say. He might spoil you too.

— Spoil me? I'm not an apple.

— Damon and Pythias, Sarkissian said. Who were they? Their names make me think of you two, anyhow.

Two days before the play their headmaster, Mr Kaul, handsome in hornrimmed specs and suede-patched tweeds, summoned them one after the other. First Jai, then the boy.

They knew his lines.

— You've got to stop meeting, your friendship is causing talk, seniors are not supposed, fraternizing inappropriate, badabadaba.

They'd learned their own lines.

Yassuh massasuh.

— Got to stand up to them.

— Tisn't a fucking military establishment.

— Is and all. Martial law I call it. Fucking dictatorship.

— Court martial's likely.

— You know the old lezzies have been talking too.

— Don't call'em that. They're our friends.

— Sorry. I'll watch my bad mouth. It's all my fault. Give a dog a bad, and all that. I'm the one's been in trouble.

— I'll be standing by you.

— You'd better be. You swore.

— Here, take this, cut my finger. Blood promise.

— Me first.

9

The first performance of the play was on Sunday. They'd been given a dressing room to share. In the cinema that the school had rented for their gala evenings, Jayalalitha, high-breasted, rose-lipped, leered at them from fresh bright poster for the Forthcoming Attraction Kadilikaneramillai (No Time For Love). Jai's happy devil was awake and sparky: laughing, jostling the boy with a hard-angled shoulder. The boy was silent. The less he spoke, the more Jai went on babbling. They went on stage. They both looked splendid. Jai had designed his own costume. In gilt, tinsel and shining black knee-length boots, he looked like Taras Bulba. The boy had been lent the long blue brocade coat his father (slimmer then and shorter than the boy is now) was married in. And his mother had draped a turquoise turban round his bushy black hair. They reached the scene in which the Prince of Persia, disguised as an old man, tricks the captain. There'd been a change. In the new version, the captain willingly handed over the flower, and still the prince tricked him, sent him to his death sentence. The betrayal scenes were brilliant, Jai grief-stricken at first and then fiery, his rich, hoarse voice in his last solo as he dedicated his heart to his beloved a revelation. They competed, reckless, throughout the performance: Jai trying to steal the show, ridden by some new vengeful demon, the boy striving to hold back, to play down his lines.

On the second night – (it was a charity gala which many of the boys' parents, arrived here ostensibly to pick up their sons but also to avail themselves of the horse races, the boat rallies and a little mountain freshness away from their stifling lowlands, were to attend) – Jai wished him luck and gave him a rose. His eyes looked bruised. ('Easier to play a hero than a villain', Sarada wrote later in the school magazine. 'Especially when you have the best tunes. The captain often sang off-pitch, which – odd enough – made his performance more poignant. But the Prince of Persia, who only has one short solo number, managed to be the centre of the play, especially when his demeanour, contrary to the lying lines he had to declaim, showed remorse; bowed shoulders, trembling voice, and – one could almost swear one saw a string of tears running down his left cheek.') It ended with Jai's monologue. On the second night Jai improvised: shouted, in the prince's face, Traitor, traitor, what use is there now for your crocodile tears? Live embers flashing in his eyes and setting (or was that the footlights?) his teeth alight. The Prince of Persia, spectator extraordinaire of the execution he'd engineered, wiped his eye with a silk handkerchief. His blood boiling, congealing, boiling, congealing, his jaw stiff with shame. He didn't know whether the tears of remorse were the prince's or his own.

Sarkissian and Sarada had decided against the happy ending with its reconciliations. The curtain fell on the captain being led to the scaffold. Which the audience, of course, wouldn't see.

10

Early June. Sarkissian came to see him. Holidays had begun and she, who'd weathered them when she was thirteen, was immune to measles. Though his were complicated by pneumonia, which his mother said he'd got walking in the cold rain after sunset.

— She locked me up in my bedroom without food, he tells her. Fuad sneaked me in a slice of bread and some cheese and a piece of pineapple or I'd have passed out with hunger. She wouldn't say who it was who came to see her and what exactly they'd said about Jai. Just that they'd painted him as a monster. Was it you, then?

— I'm sorry. But it was she who came to see me. She stopped by on the way back from market, she said. But she was on foot. Said she'd had an unsigned note. From the school. About Jai.

— What did you say?

— That they were saying he'd harm you.

— Who said that?

— Well, Sarada.

— Did she send the note?

— I don't know. Yes . . .

— You know about him and Kamalak . . .

— Yes. Hush, child. It was you I really cared about. Didn't want you to be hurt. But he's the one I really hurt. Did you tell him?

— How could I? You know Ma made me swear never to speak to him again? On Daddy's life? What was in that note?

— Oh my dearest boy, that it should be me who has to tell you all this. That you and he had unhealthy feelings. Unnatural. That you indulged in unnatural practices. And that in your position – as the son of an enemy alien – you and your parents wouldn't want any trouble, we had to be particularly cautious in our handling of you. Oh, that I of all people should have to report this to you . . . (Melodrama, the only appropriate reaction to her own words, creasing her brow, making her wring her hands.)

— You read all that? And you didn't . . .

— I said that in such confined environments younger boys were often lead astray by older boys so you couldn't be too careful. She said you'd had trouble with a cousin and her older boyfriend of another faith. I said that some boys were trouble and Jai had had his share of that. Kamalakshi. Mani. The devil in Jai's eyes . . . you know what they say. Everyone has a devil in a box; but you have to learn to sit on it . . . But it's your devil I'm worried about now. He's set you on fire. Look at your skin. (Running a thin yellow hand through his uncombed black thatch.) It'll probably scar.

— The doctor said measles rarely do. But what do I do now?

(O Stella, sister of the rocks, star of the sea, did you do this to teach me to sit still, you who left Calcutta in pursuit of your lady weasel, and spent twenty-two years of joy in a boat in the blue and diamond-studded sky, has losing your sweet Molly made you so careless and unkind?) How do I tell him? And I know you've been pilfering lines from detective fiction. Gladys Mitchell. I borrowed *Devil's Elbow* after you.

— You can't, not now. I will. He's still here you know. The seniors are still doing their tutorials. I'm going up on Saturday to give him his piano lesson, I'll tell him. It's the least I can do.

. . . *So you want to play Dame Beatrice, now, do you? Save the criminal you've decided should be let off the hook?*

. . . *What's more important – a vow on your father's life or a promise made on mingled blood from scratched fingertips?*

11

On Midsummer's Eve Mack swallowed all the painkillers in the house and died that night. Stella Sarkissian said she'd turned down his proposal. She'd thought it a tipsy joke. (They'd opened Molly's last bottle of Bristol Cream earlier in the evening: it would have been Molly's birthday.) People say: That howling jackal of a mountain monsoon wind drives at least one Brit mad each year. (Who knows why, their own weather was bad enough, if they'd wanted warm weather they should've stayed down in the plains.) They laid him to sleep in sweet Molly's grave. He'd had it dug deep enough for two.

The boy spent a lot of time with Stella that summer. Watching her paint, or listening to her melancholy music. She told him Jai had only said to her: So you've seen him? And then added, OK, so I understand.

The boy sat for hours in the library when he had time to himself (which was all he seemed to have these days after Fuad, bored witless by his cousin's surly moods, had left for Bombay). Vans drove up to the house: the horses were carried away and the stables left empty. Dad was giving up horseflesh only a year after starting his enterprise. I'm not a businessman, he said with remorse: he'd been allowing his city friends, princes and politicians, to forget about the bills he ought to have sent them in the first place for the servicing and the upkeep of their beasts. He left for Bombay with Fuad. See you soon, he said, but his first letter to his son made it clear he wasn't planning on returning. So it was to be the boy, his mother, and Rehmat the maid for the next year and a half, alone in the pisshole and living on remittances, red beans and curds and thick rice, escaping perhaps for short holidays by the sea.

Summer in the mountains brought a hard rain down. It fell like darts. Sometimes the town was calf-deep in bilge and he couldn't navigate the tricky paths. He'd stay at home for three days at a time, light a fern-smelling fire with twigs he'd gathered, and read about Chopin and George Sand, D'Annunzio, Duse and Wilde and Isadora. Vanessa Redgrave, whom he'd just seen as Guinevere, gave birth to a son without being married. He pinned up a poster of her (arms folded modestly over her bare breasts and hair flowing in arty disarray around her strong bones) over his bed. No protest from Ma: she probably thought he was forgetting Jai. Sometimes, in the evenings, as she sat by the fire he'd made, he'd make her read out passages from the stories by Ismat Chughtai and Qurratulain Hyder she loved and ask her the meanings of words obscure to him. He was beginning to feel that the sound of his mother tongue was becoming so unfamiliar he'd forget it soon, as he'd almost forgotten, while he struggled to master the alien Hindi alphabet, how to read and write his own. The pit of loneliness Dad's leaving had dug in their earth was making them allies, if not friends.

But he wasn't forgetting Jai. He wrote the first of his letters in mid-July and hid it in Isadora Duncan's *My Life*, which he'd bought from Higginbothams with his pocket money on the way to the Assembly Rooms where they were showing *The Fugitive Kind* for just one day. He told Jai how he'd come home that night and found his mother waiting on the porch, how she'd told him one of the teachers had been to see her with a message from the school, he'd thought it was Sarkissian but he knew now it was Sarada, how she'd said she'd heard their friendship was dangerous.

He didn't talk about the other things – those unsayable words, unnatural, unhealthy – but he wrote.

12

21 August 1969

Jai,

I've sworn to my mother on my father's life I'll never say a word to you again. But I didn't say a thing about writing. So I'm not breaking a promise like I broke mine to you which I'm trying to honour now. Sarkissian says she's told you everything. Is there any chance at all that the valiant captain will – just once more – pardon the treacherous Prince of Persia? I'll understand if you don't but I beg you to write to me. Just once. And if you don't just let me keep on writing to you.

Your friend forever

S.

25 August 1969

Dear S. ,

I got your note. I understand everything now. You were in trouble. It was a long summer, without knowing what had happened. I guessed but I thought it might be something wrong I had done. Then Sarkissian told me you'd talked to her. Thank you for the book which I found on the piano stool. What a surprise to find your note hidden inside it. You are one clever beggar. Listen, meet me in the playing field after sports on Friday if you can hang around in the library till then and come up the hill the back way. You can't talk to me but I can still talk to you.

Your loving friend

Jai

P. S.   I think Isadora D. was one hell of a fascinating dame, but that Yesenin, he was nuts. Seriously.

13

They meet in the playfield. And then in the lab. At a time Jai gives him.

— We have to watch it. Not give ourselves away. I've got to get through this year. My final exams. Can't afford to mess it up.

The boy can't answer. So he nods. He smells Jai's fear, fighting the formaldehyde. Dead saurians smile at them from glass cases. A desiccated rabbit lies on the central table.

Sometimes he lets Jai hold his hands, but he doesn't really like Jai to touch him, because it brings back the fear he felt of Jai, and the shame, when he heard from Sarkissian about the lies, the allegations; even more, because it brings back Mani, and he doesn't want to be another Mani.

∾⊛∾

September. Silence now where once there was singing. You have to fill the hollows with sound.

Sometimes you speak aloud to yourself like the habitually lonely. But then you've never been much of a talker. So it's easier to write: when you go home, despairing, knowing your one friend's been taken from you, you'd barely realized how precious it all was when it was taken away so what was the point, you sit down at your table, try to put it all in words, and it flows. Like music. You can hear the notes. Fireflies of sound just beyond your reach. Flashing by too fast for you to catch. But you're trying. Your body aches and strains but at the same time you're like a lame man dancing. Your feet tap as you strive to catch those red notes, like fireflies in a jar, you sway and rise and bend, sway and rise and bend. Then you weigh your wings and you leave your bones behind and you're there. For an instant. With the fireflies. Before you fall.

So much to tear up, throw away, so much you can never tell him, tell anyone: but when you write there's a Jai beyond the shoulder of the grim-faced man-boy he's become, worrying himself to a skeleton about his results, beyond the Jai who you know will leave you and this pisshole to go back to his island in the sea.

You write to a Jai who's even beyond the Jai that waits for you and writes back to you, sometimes two notes for each one you send him, who flinches when you can't answer his questions and says: We'd better split before someone sees us. You write to his shadow-brother, to the Jai who could have been, if they'd let him keep on singing his ditties to you, in unison or in harmony, you write to the sea captain who brought you, here in the mountains, a catamaran from China, which they smashed and burnt, making a bonfire which still sends up rank smoke fumes that foul this air.

∽ ❀ ∽

October. Evenings fell early. The sun had been on sabbatical for days; the dark grey sky was in turmoil. Lowering clouds, like buffalo herds, seemed to loll for hours in the lake. The water was dark, turbulent: it hadn't been blue for a month, not even in daylight. The early signs of morning frost made the uphill walks hazardous. Rehmat the maidservant said the lake was claiming lives again. Two peasants had drowned in it last week. Someone said they were lovers. A married Brahmin woman whose husband had been away for months, pregnant with her Badaga lover's baby, threw herself in first. Then the Badaga lover, who heard her call for him every night for eleven days until he followed her.

∽ ❀ ∽

You write. You can't stop. You copy out the few lines that say enough without saying too much, carefully fold away what you won't give him now, to read later, to try and understand. You follow his tone and he follows yours, it's a dizzy dance, of jokes, banter and half-truths – but the sight of his words on paper, before the deadening feeling that words will never fill the hole you feel inside, sends a thrill up your skull like the sharp scent of a night-flower, so he must feel the same. Sometimes your notes cross and you find you've both written, word for word, the same sentence. Sometimes you sit for what seems like hours rewriting in your mind the messages he's sent you, and you'll feel you're almost there, in his skin, in his sinews, feeling what he felt when he wrote to you, recognizing his eyes in the gaps, as you hope he'll see yours in the words you've rubbed out. But it's a bold act, that, a trespass, to be forbidden, an invasion, of a private territory of muscle and bone.

Then there's the danger: of being found out, caught, which you can sense inspires him and holds him back in turn, fights with his fear of

*being expelled again, a fear which you – who no longer have anything
to lose in this prison, who don't want to stay to see him leave, who want
to be expelled, that's the challenge – you don't feel. But you see how it's
changed him, made him weak and contrite, in awe of authority, like a
clerk in a grey-and-white film. You can't imagine what it'll be like when
he's left, when your half-life will turn into no life, and your devil will be
chained to a boulder in the deep sea. But you know that he can't wait to
escape, his devil's only sleeping in a box, and when he's with you it
awakens in him, kicks and shouts, but he stifles it, strangles it, sits on it
for his own sake and for yours. You don't want to know what you know,
but you do: his need to reach out to you is filling him with shame.*

And you write.

14

November. Nearly three months of occasional and furtive meetings.
Hastier, each time, more tense, with a greater sense of something left
unfinished. The boy didn't know how long he could stay mute. Jai was
leaving in December, after finishing his Senior Cambridge exams. A
relief, in a way, because then, at last, the silence the boy had imposed
on himself would be substituted for a silence imposed by time. What
life would be like, here in the school, in the hills, next year, with Jai
gone, he couldn't bear to imagine. But before that new year came, they
were going to Bombay, for a month: Dad had sent tickets, they were
taking the train from Coimbatore before Christmas.

It was a month of festivals. Lamps were lit one night. By the huge
bonfire in the school's courtyard, Saradakka sang in a low lush voice,
a Kannada song about sunflowers, her notes weaving round their
heads like a hummingbird's wings. Then there was a chorus from the
Kerala boys, a shrimp-boat song from the popular movie Chemmeen,
and Jai, looking lively for once, as he had when he led the Devil's
Stones, sang with them. The boy sang, too: Black is the colour of my

true love's hair. Tonight they were all saying goodbye to Stella who was leaving soon for Calcutta to join the brother she'd seen only rarely in the last twenty years. She was sick of this town, the boy knew that. Of its belly, distended with the grief of the armless beggars and the potato-field prostitutes and the monkeys and the wind whining over the murky lake. You can't call a place home more than twice, and if you've made your home in someone's heart and that heart stopped beating an age ago, what happens then to the place you learnt to call home? Silence where once you played songs. She didn't need to say these things: he'd seen them in her eyes.

That night, with lamps ablaze and the feel of festivities around them, no one could stop him from being with Jai. No one would even notice. Following an intuition – or observing, from the corner of his eye, that Jai had been absent for a quarter of an hour – he went to the lab. Jai was there, waiting.

In the garden, the early frost had bitten off the edges of magnolias and killed the camellias. He got home late that night; it was nearly nine. He'd taken a yellow taxi. At the door, he saw Rehmat weeping. Don't worry, she said, there's news from Bombay, the Master . . . He pushed past her into the sitting room, where his mother was sitting by the fireplace in her usual high chair, though there wasn't a fire. You'd better get your things packed, she said, we're taking the plane from Coimbatore the day after tomorrow. A month early? he said irrelevantly. It's only November. She handed him the telegram. Carefully worded, from Fuad's father, her eldest brother, in Bombay. Dad was in hospital. He'd had a heart attack three days ago, nothing to worry about, but they were needed there, Dad was missing them, he'd asked about them. The boy knew that without being told.

15

Four of them took the toy train from Mettupalayam two days later: the boy, his mother, Rehmat and her infant daughter. In the end, the maid had wept so much that Ma couldn't bear to leave her behind. Ma had been packing up the few things she'd brought to the blue mountains for days, so Rehmat, say what Ma might, had been convinced they were leaving for ever. What will become of me, Ma? she'd harrowingly cried. How can you leave me here? And when Ma had told her, too, to gather up her child and her belongings and travel with them – she'd be better off, with a job in Bombay – the boy had wondered whether he dare hope that they wouldn't be coming back.

— So in the end, you're leaving before both of us, said Stella, who was at the station to see them off. Jai said to wish you luck.

Seen from the train the town, as it fell and shrunk behind them, reminded him, as always, of a landscape enclosed in a paperweight. He'd had no time to say goodbye to Jai. Not even to write a note. In the worry and the frenzy of timetables and departures, it hadn't been on his mind. As they left the villa, it had only occurred to him that he'd forgotten to go to the English cemetery with Stella and a parting bouquet for the Macks, and that if the blue flowers had blossomed last summer it must have been the week he'd lain quarantined with measles because he never had seen the old bones of the mountains turn blue.

Painting on Glass

Last night: I was at the South Bank to see a Malay film I had been asked to review. The blurb for it had announced serious themes, fundamentalism and feminism and polygyny and Palestinian refugees, but what we saw was a work full of vitality, of romance and butterflies and reconciliations. I struggled with cynicism and suspended it, thinking of the challenge and the problems of presenting a message to a mass audience in a 'developing' country, of addressing issues and causes in a coherent voice, treading the tightrope between the aesthetic and the popular and paying homage to both . . . but each clumsy cut, each musical interlude and sentimental gesture was greeted with a chorus of catcalls and guffaws by an audience that didn't know when to laugh and when to cry.

As I left the theatre and walked towards the bridge that leads to Embankment station I jingled the coins in my pocket, ready for the hungry hands and eyes of the homeless that haunt the narrow path. At least I'd buy a *Big Issue* for the tube ride home. There but for fortune, I often think. It was raining, an untimely grey early June drizzle. The surging sound of a saxophone stopped me and I turned to look: a woman was dancing to the music of a cassette recorder, dancing with her eyes closed and tossing a red rag from her hand up into the air like a weightless partner, dancing ecstatic and shockingly alone. I don't know what her dancing did to me, but suddenly I wanted to be by myself. I wanted to be at home, and I ran. It wasn't even dark yet but

the clouds had swallowed the sunset for supper and the river was the
colour of dishwater.

I don't know why I'm writing all this but since Tahira left for
Karachi I've been going a lot to the cinema on my own and thinking
of the films and the music she liked. And of the story she'd asked me
to write about my life and send to Pakistan for her to publish in her
journal; everything I see and hear seems to flow into it. I wanted to
write something spare and stark and simple because over the last few
years I've always thought that simplicity speaks to the widest possible
audience, but the film I'd seen made me think again. I wondered what
Tahira would have said about it, what she'd have said to the woman
who'd directed it, how they'd have talked about Islam, censorship,
roots and social responsibility. I thought about the films made by
Asians here, those tales of estrangement and compromise, *Samosas on
the Sand* and *Tennessee Tandoori* and *Croydon Country Singers* and
The Krishna of the Counties, how I'd colluded in her mocking
comments about them until I realized that she saw me, too, as an
alienated migrant cut off from my roots, and I knew that she was
waiting for me to prove myself with something new, something
authentic. I began to think about the heaviness of trees: in our
country, in our verses, we talk about the displaced as birds without
wings, birds who can no longer fly to their destination, and words
about roots and sources began to disturb me. Because trees have
heavy bodies; a tree removed from its native soil and planted
elsewhere puts down new roots, twisted ones, perhaps, but its trunk
grows heavy. You try to leave and something pulls at you, the earth
holds you back. The soil of a new language and new necessities. I
thought of the day I'd walked down Guildford Street on my way to
Russell Square and seen a dead rat thrown out on the pavement, and
that evening a pigeon, mangled, red and crushed, lay on what I could
swear was the very same spot. I began to wish I could find my lost sky,
my horizon, my lost words. Films and television have taken over from
painters and poets, and we're all left stranded with dead images like
piles of dead leaves, dead butterflies, dead birds. Robbed of their

source in a living language. I've always held that art should be both beautiful and useful, but when in doubt I've usually thrown the beauty out. Though perhaps the way to reach people is to talk in those primary colours that this wretched drizzle seems to wash away, to fill stories with light and animation and so what if the audience laughs at the tragic moments: let the emotions spill over the top, and maybe the happy scenes and gestures will make them cry. Simplicity rests in the pact – I've been there, I know – between the teller and listener, not in sentence structures or narrative lines. People recognize and relate to complications and clutter – after all, they're what make up our lives. It's the content that matters, in the end. Perhaps it's innocence we laugh at, the innocence of belief, but we long for it too, the mess and the muddle and the ache of betrayal.

Enough rambling, enough reflection. Let's get on with it, let me tell you about my life. My name is Irfan Malik. I've been in London eight years. I was born in Pakistan thirty-six years ago and grew up in Lahore. I took a couple of degrees there and after doing a stint at an advertising agency I went into journalism, working for television and co-editing a popular fortnightly English review. I also wrote poetry and TV plays in Urdu and Punjabi and published a book about the things I saw and I knew, about my grandparents' village and about the city and love and corruption and change, the usual bourgeois stuff, you could say, but it was what I loved doing and it brought me some applause, and also some censure from my politically correct mates but even they said I had a flair for words and images.

I don't really suppose that I was a great success as a Pakistani man – poetry and such are hardly the material middle-class parents' dreams are made of – but I'm a second son and it didn't really matter. My elder brother went abroad to study medicine and my parents couldn't afford to send me overseas, anyway. I made some kind of independent living. But when my chance came I took it, and you could say my chance was engineered by my parents. And Aneela's. She was the daughter of distant relatives. Attractive, brilliantly well educated by anyone's standards, she came to Lahore on what we used to call a shopping trip at college and chose me as the asset she was shopping for. She was on the rebound; her long relationship with an Americanized Pakistani had broken, I was a relative of respectable origins, and she said she loved my love poems – I wrote one about our second meeting which was, well, intense. She was an odd mixture of chic and sluttish and that seemed sophisticated and ineffably foreign to me. Her father had a newspaper chain in London as a tax outlet and they'd opened an English section, a serious political and cultural review. I would be perfect as its acting editor: I had the experience and the talent.

So it was London for me. An approved rather than an arranged marriage. The in-laws' house in Bramham Gardens – which they insisted was in South Ken, though it's actually Earls Court – and the office and my book of verse published in Lahore clutched under my arm and Third World poetry readings which my journal's budget occasionally allowed me to organize. I met poets from Africa and Latin America and the Arab world and sometimes they invited me to read with them. London was still political in those days, at least in its Third World peripheries, and Marxism hadn't yet become a bad smell. I knew my poems occasionally aroused a frown or worse still a sneer, which was strange, because it made me realize that though I hadn't been particularly aware of it I'd been speaking to an international audience all the time, and international meant English-speaking. No one was desperate to translate my work so I found myself dealing, to what I now see as my detriment, with a new language. I'd somehow mixed up the translations of Neruda and Paz I'd read with English poetry, which I knew almost nothing about, but that, that was another world altogether, and the dark-skinned poets I met here in our segregated enclaves were angry.

Really angry. About imperialism and exploitation and racism. I learned their language: I began to write protest poetry too. After all, I was, by their admission, a man of the Third World, and I came from a country in the metal grasp of a military apparatus. Once an English patron of writers of colour, slightly the worse for drink, accused me of being, as a Pakistani, a partisan of oppression and Islam and misogyny because I made the mistake of telling her to accept an invitation to speak about her writing in a British Council tour of Pakistan. Those were the days of the Rushdie affair and it wasn't exactly chic to be Pakistani or Muslim. I responded for once in that angry manner with which I was becoming familiar. And what about your fucking Tories, I said. They've got you all by the balls and none of you even admits that there are beggars and homeless around everywhere on your streets. I had my material – you only had to read an article about Pakistan or watch a documentary to get it – and I had apartheid, intifada, Ethiopia, Timor and Tiananmen to supplement that. We carry our histories on our backs, I wrote, in our blood and in our bones. But at the same time I knew somewhere in these bones of mine that what we were doing was only ranting and raving and preaching to each other and to the ranks of the already rallied, our words wouldn't get us to where we really wanted to go, our well of words was running out of fresh water as if a cow or worse still a pig had died in it. That we didn't have the courage to face an era which had placed us in a safe asylum, where we could scream the screams of dumb bright birds just as long as we didn't make a noise in the neighbourhood, disturb the local residents by shattering the glass walls of our aviary.

And then, four years after I came here, things fell apart.

My father-in-law was accused – rightly or wrongly – of malpractices in his business dealings and had to run. His empire was frozen and the newspaper chain bought out. Looking back at that time I wonder if I put it into words then what I know now: we'd never really belonged as an elite, we'd only lived here in a replica of our ways at home or as a distorted reflection of the West's well-off. As long as they could bear us in their midst. But at some time, as the tide of financial return went down lower and lower our status as a class within a class had to change, too. Someone brought down an axe to break our mirror and it's no use citing conspiracy theories and Western fears of Third World gain and prosperity to explain our downfall by degrees.

My marriage had frozen, too, in its second year, and though we remained quite civilized with each other and still slept together desultorily Aneela and I led our own lives. Aneela hadn't ever got over her great love and her vodka drinking became hazardous. Most of the time she was a good enough mother to our little daughter and it was Suhayla that kept us together – still does, in a way. It was understood before I moved myself and my abilities to London that I'd be improving my educational qualifications here. And my abilities, it emerged, were negligible in Aneela's eyes, since she'd never managed to mould me into the model of moneyed manhood she'd imagined. My decision to take a degree in history rather than the MBA she was insisting I should do made me look to her even more like the under-achieving wimp she already thought I was. I got my Master's from evening classes at Birkbeck. She'd thought it would be better to do a course in journalism, at least, and maybe she was right; I realized that when I found myself a sojourner on the swelling tide of unemployment. When I couldn't find anything else someone suggested I take a course in English as a Second Language which the redundancy money that had somehow come my way from the liquidators helped to fund. So there I was, at thirty-two, with a bagful of qualifications none of which amounted to very much, and I'd realized long ago that I certainly wasn't the poet of the age. I knew, though, that I wasn't bad either: that was proved when a Caribbean publisher as well respected for his radical politics as for his generous and tough aesthetic commissioned a collection of my London work. He brought out a slim volume called *After the Death of Zia, Thatcher and Reagan* a year after Aneela left for Boston, her lover and yet another redundant degree. She's never done a thing with her hopes or her high educational achievements.

I was a grass widower. Aneela hadn't talked about divorce, maybe for Suhayla's sake. We clung together for a bit like rain-drenched children and seemed to be sexually alive to each other like we'd been before. Then one night I heard her telling her best friend on the phone how her lover had rung her up for a drink while he was passing through town and she couldn't resist seeing him, telling herself it was only a greeting for the sake of the past, then in the deserted hotel bar late that winter night he'd touched her as if they were in bed again, she'd found herself half-undressed right there on the sofa and when she told him to stop he left her there, like that, humiliated but alive again or half-alive, because the part of her that he'd left behind was dead, had been dead for so long, and the part of herself she'd shared with me was dying now. I never told her that I'd heard but she knew that I knew it was really over. She said when she left that she only wanted to clear her head and I pretended I believed she'd be back soon. Suhayla cried a lot when we said goodbye but I let her go because I knew that with the life ahead of me I couldn't afford to look after her or give her the things she was used to. Soon after they went I moved from Earls Court to a short life flat in EC1 a classmate from my ESL group was vacating to move to Australia: bedsit and attached bath and no cooking facilities, only a single ring on which I could boil water for tea or an egg and use as a heater when it got too cold. I could barely afford even that. I came to know every chip shop in the area and when the grungy walls sang dirges to me I sat for hours with elbows on sticky white tables over a paper glass of Coke at Burger King with strobe lights in my eyes.

When I felt really hollow those things about Aneela that I'd taken for granted, those cheating memories, perhaps, from which we sketch our similes, trickled down my face like sweat in the hot lights: the feeling of her nipples and the underslopes of her breasts beneath my fingers and how her back warmed against me as she fell asleep, the thought of her hands and how, when I turned away from her in sleepy forgetfulness, she'd run her fingers down from the bones above my chest to my sex and back up again until every bit of me, even the hairs on my body, woke up. You remember those things more vividly than lovemaking when you lose them.

Going back to Lahore was out and I never even considered it. My doctor father had retired years ago and moved to Rawalpindi to be close to my brother and his family who'd settled in Islamabad, which was strange to me. I'd only visited them there a couple of times since my marriage. I suppose I understand now why I didn't leave London: damaged goods can be returned to their sellers and their makers, but what about goods that are damaged on the way, or broken by their buyers? Who'll want to have those back? I think that's how I felt. Why the hell should Pakistan want me, the mediocre editor of a small-circulation Third World journal, a little-known poet who'd long ago lost touch with home, with a degree in history which wasn't even a doctorate? What would I do there – teach English as a second language to the children of the rich who'd grown up speaking English anyway? Anyone who left a home will know what it's like to go back with nothing gained, a supplicant rather than an achiever. At least I was an absolute stranger here, incomer, outsider, and I was only reclaiming the money I'd poured into some robot machine's pockets for so many bloody years. I haven't ever been back since things went wrong. Somewhere, within me, the sleeping poetry said no, no, no.

And the Third World coterie for which I'd read my poetry had gone, too, in search of higher ground. Now I did classrooms, community centres, backwood bookshops and questions I couldn't answer. My poetic urge had been flagging for aeons, it was arthritic now. I didn't have much of a sense of community here, and you need to write from a sense of something. I couldn't keep on singing about kite festivals, first love, my daughter, Aung San Suu Kyi or South Africa. A culture had grown up among the second generation of subcontinental immigrants that I hadn't really had the time or the inclination to understand: bhangra discos and Joy Bangla and boots under shalwars and Hindi movie stars. Aneela'd said it was all a distorted copy of the real thing; I'd say now there's more to it than that. But at the time, I'd just been too busy and preoccupied with the journal, the organization of functions and readings and Third World conferences, fatherhood, Aneela's complaint that motherhood and a busy, busy husband were cannibalizing her youth . . . You could have called me self-centred, if I'd ever had enough of a self to consider. I'd just spent my life at the office and used to come home to fall into bed six days a week, and on Sundays I'd take Suhayla out and watch videos and read the papers.

When I thought the Job Centre people would shoot me if I stood in their queues for another handout, when the Third World editor-friends and favour-owers of another time had run out of all the book reviews, dance reviews, film reviews, theatre reviews and ultimately even race and public march and issue reviews, all the commissions they could give me at diminishing fees (from £70 down to £20), when even a can of beans cost too much and I'd gone down two stones in weight and owed £340 I didn't have, I found myself at Brickenshore College, Brickenshore, London, a teacher of ESL to refugees from Ethiopia, China, Iran and Vietnam. Not exactly what I'd envisaged. Three years on I'm still there, but don't feel for a moment that it's taught me a thing. I don't feel close to them, I don't feel they allay my sense of having lost my place; all I feel is heavy, a heavy trunk with withered bark and hanging branches and leaves that fall in thick, yellow piles before they ever grow. When I first joined and planned my lessons according to my ESL teacher's careful briefing, two of the students – a Laotian and Chinese – began to shout at me, told me they didn't want to learn silly, pretty things, only useful English to help them with a trade. I wanted to leave. But the Eritreans and the Poles – one of them was much older than me – wanted me to stay. And I did. For the money, for a place in life, to make sense of the heaviness of me. Work that was ugly but useful. Unlike this story of my life: ugly and of no use at all.

But that's not what Tahira would say. Tahira, who suddenly reappeared after years during my Easter holidays. I'd arranged a poetry reading here for her once, in my editorial days. She'd filled the hall with her poems. She was radical and lyrical and illuminating. And intimidating. You felt she was meeting us expatriates on sufferance. Later, though, when we'd met again, she was under some sort of political cloud, had published things she shouldn't, and had come here to see if she could reroute, or reroot herself, find something in this otherwhere. But her roots weren't portable. We needed each other: she a rudder in a strange land, me someone that reminded me of my dreaming days. Sometimes I think it wasn't my age or her pain or her need for friendship over intensity and passion that stopped her listening to my starving eyes. It was the call of a sky far way, it was her revolt against this alien sky. She told me I should start writing in Urdu again, writing for Pakistan, as a way, perhaps, of coming back for a while. I even think of it now: returning in anonymity, going to rest for a while with my parents, and then taking a backpack and going far, far up into the hills, starting off with Margalla. Then I'll go to Karachi to see Tahira. Because she went back. To the pain of her new wings growing, to the heaviness of her tree. Asking me to write, as soon as I could, about my life here, in English if I couldn't find the Urdu words and she'd translate it. So I began, hacking away at my bark and carving into it the initials of someone who's desired more than he's done and known longing more than love and never loved enough, someone who's tried to write without living and turned his face away from everyone for fear of being hurt, someone who's spent his days with his face pressed to glass and never learned to move or break the glass walls of his cage, like a bird that lost its tree and ended up in an aviary, or a tree that never grew branches to make a home for birds.

Mixed metaphors. Windows and walls. When I first started teaching I used to walk past a blind wall. It served no purpose, led nowhere, concealed nothing. Over the months, the graffiti on it kept changing: first it was WHOSA COMIN? SOCHY LIZM I'S A COMIN in huge letters and I used to wonder who Sochy was. Then it was KILROY WAS 'ERE. I hated the wall, because sometimes it reminded me of my attempts at poetry, writing loud protest at first and later merely trying to remind people I existed and myself that I had a name. Then one day the authorities decided to do something about it and instead of breaking it down they got a team of painters to make a mural, a gaudy scene of fake optimism with smiling children and giant daisies and daffodil sunshine. It used to make me feel like banging my head in misery because those colours were so false and heavy, purples and dingy oranges and peacock blues, and it made me want to turn away and say to hell with the job which as I write I'm probably about to lose anyway. Without redundancy money because I've only been employed on annual contracts for the three years I've been there.

Last night – this morning, really, because I'd been working on the fragment about my life well after midnight – I fell asleep and dreamed that the wall with its ghastly mural was blocking the view from my window and I had to get up to wipe off the bright paint and break it down. I took a bucket full of water and some washcloths downstairs to do the job but when I got there I found that I'd taken a bucket of paint instead and what I had to do was cover the tawdry hope on the wall with new pictures. I was about to begin when I woke up, sweating. I went to the window and of course there was no wall but the sky was heavy and grey again. The computer clock said 7:45. A June Sunday. For some reason it occurred to me that if the weather had been like that when I was in Pakistan I'd have rung up some friends and we'd have gone on a picnic, to the hills from Lahore or Islamabad, far, far out to the clean sea from Karachi. The wall was still with me and I knew what I had to do. I looked at the bald words I'd written and I sat down to write again, something for Tahira's magazine but even more for myself, from my own pleasure and pain, a dream story like those pieces Pakistani writers used to write during Zia's regime, couched in disturbing similes, in the colours of unease. My window had been, after all, my cage and my wall, keeping me from breathing, and I should write about that. As I wrote, rapidly, from right to left, the syllables of my lost tongue licked my skin like fires.

In my story, a young painter meets an alluring pair, a wise old man and his beautiful daughter, from a land across the sea. He falls in love with the daughter and apprentices himself to the old man who is one of his time's greatest painters. He follows them abroad. But when he reaches the strange city of his destination they take him to the top of a tower to a great room made of glass, overlooking the steeples and the spires and the rivers of the alien city. He is left with one brush and pots of paints and locked into the room. The old man tells him he must paint a living masterpiece on the glass walls within eleven days, when they will come back to redeem him: only then will he be worthy of their esteem, the old man's tutelage, the young woman's love. He starts on the third day, after three days of desolation. He begins from the right corner, painting a street of the city of his exile, a street he can only see from the distance of his fourteenth-floor room over rooftops and chimneys. A river runs around the room. Down a tree-lined avenue, a loving couple walk: he small and slender, she tall and very, very fat. On the platform of a little station stands a young man from the Far East, with a finger in his ear. On another street corner there's a pub, with a bench outside and a young ginger-headed man sitting on it with a giant mug of beer in his left hand. He looks at a girl who throws in the air a red scarf, dancing, dancing. Two children, a boy and a girl, point an airgun at a pigeon in a tree.

When the painter stops painting, the glass walls are nearly covered: the setting sun's rays bring everything to life, colours dance around him, their tones rebelling against the shades he's chosen. But there's still a lack. Who, he asks himself, is looking at all this: where is the centre of my scene? His paints are finished: he will have to use the yields of his body, blood and sweat and other, darker fluids. His fine brush is broken. He paints with his fingers. At the top right-hand corner of the room he paints a giant tree, gnarled, rich with green leaves: the home of birds, sparrows and humble flying things, even butterflies, though he wonders if butterflies can actually reach its branches. He stops, and looks at his work. Perhaps he sleeps for a while, for when he comes back to himself he's on the street, seated beneath his tree. He begins to walk. As he passes the pub, the ginger-haired man, now flushed with beer, spits twice, once to the right of the painter's right shoe, once to the left of his left shoe. The painter walks on. The pigeon has fallen from its tree, shot by the playful children; it lies in a knot of blood and sinew and feather and bone. He walks on. The red dancer has gone. A saxophonist stands in her place, playing music that reminds him of fire in an autumn garden. Faces he hasn't painted assail him. A young man accosts him and asks: Do you want to do business? Business? he says, and he wonders whether the young man will set him up as a pavement artist, for he knows he is dreaming, and in dreams people read your mind. But I want to sell you my corpse, says the young man, because I got off a ship from Romania ten days ago and I need money for cigarettes and new shoes. But I don't want your body, the painter says, and I have nothing to give you, my table is bare, my pockets are empty. He walks on, but his footsteps are faster. At the next corner he sees the fat woman. Her thin lover lies on the stones with blood on his forehead. Seated on his chest, the woman batters with her fists her lover's shoulders, chanting all the while: But I love you, you swine, you bastard. I do, I love you. The painter walks on. The man from the East who stood smiling on the platform stands outside the station now. He looks at what he finds in his ears, blows gently, and repeats the gesture: now he explores his nose, now he picks at his scalp, always blowing, blowing at his fingers. He asks the painter for a cigarette. I have nothing, says the painter, I am a stranger here. Then you can have one of my films, says the man from the East handing him a parcel, because I like you am a stranger, and since we can't pay for women to love, my two friends and I watch images of other people making love every night when we go home from work in the restaurant kitchen, to the attic room we share. I don't want your film, the painter says. He walks on. He's back at the tree where he started, but his shoes are heavy with mulch, and the season must have changed, for piles of leaves lie beneath the tree, nesting small dead things. He stops. The shadows of the city fall on him through the glass. His painting sleeps again. He is breathless, exhausted. He knows his eleven days are over now. No one has come to redeem him. He knows now that the woman who had enchanted him was the old man's lover, not his daughter. The old man will teach him nothing. He's a captive in this glass tower. The colours of the street he has painted, painted on glass, are fading. Forms merge with the deepening night. He clings to the tree, drawing on its heaviness for succour, but it's only a tracery of painted lines on glass. Then he hears thunder, and a crack of blue lightning hits the window. Branches push against the glass, looking for rain and light. He hears the glass smash about him. The tower falls but that doesn't matter. Warm drops of light shower my bark, the rain pours its blue sap on me. My tree still stands. Green leaves burst from my skin, green shoots explode from me. Rivulets of light run through my fingers. I hear the sound of wings in my ears as migrant birds on their way to the south make their nests in my green head. In anticipation of the deluge, I raise my hands. My fresh raw limbs reach outwards, to talk to the punishing and the pardoning sky.

Acknowledgements and Author's Note

Some of these stories have previously appeared in the following antho-logies and journals:

'Painting on Glass' and 'Sweet Rice' in *Leave to Stay* (Virago 1996); 'This other Salt' in *Trafika*, 1995; 'The Lost Cantos of the Silken Tiger' in *Dragonfly in the Sun*, (OUP Karachi, 1997); 'Benedetta, Amata' in *11 Tolomeo* (Venice 1998). 'Painting on Glass' also appeared in *Fires in an Autumn Garden* (OUP Karachi 1997); and 'Sweet Rice' in *Kunapipi*, 1998.

I particularly wish to thank Shirley Chew, Joan Riley, Asif Farrukhi and Muneeza Shamsie for eliciting stories. I'm also grateful to Asif, Muneeza and Fahmida Riaz for making my trip to Karachi so stimulating, and for keeping me connected to our city.

I'd also like to acknowledge an award of £1,500 from the Society of Authors in 1994 to begin this book.

I'm grateful to Jenny Stringer for her eagle eye and editorial finesse.

Mimi Khalvati and Bun Bahng were enthusiastic readers throughout 1995, Amit Chaudhuri read the first completed manuscript, and last but by no means least Kamila Shamsie proved the ideal reader as the book went to press: I'd like to thank you all.

For those of you who want to know, Muhammadi Begum and Rafi Ajmeri (my maternal great-uncle), are historical characters.

Two final words of thanks.

Mai Ghoussoub has been involved with this book since I wrote its third story, and it would probably have taken much longer to appear if she hadn't been so passionate in her nagging.

My mother Sabiha, from whom I inherited my love of words and music, and an entire heritage of stories: this book is dedicated to you with my gratitude and love.

Aamer Hussein
London, April 1999

Hoops of Fire
Fifty Years of Fiction by Pakistani Women

Edited by
Aamer Hussein

As the fires of partition consume a recently decolonized populace and new borderlines are drawn on maps, a young woman is abducted to spend a life in exile; in the beautiful hill country, a naive peasant is left with a white man's baby; a middle-class housewife sees visions of salvation in the tricks of circus animals . . .

In this collection of stories by Pakistan's finest women writers – including Jamila Hashmi, Mumtaz Shirin, Khadija Mastur, Khalida Husain and Fahmida Riaz – we are introduced to the intricate narrative patterns and compelling cadences of a rich literary culture which deserves to be better known. Spanning the entire fifty years of a new nation's history, and ranging in style from harsh realism to poetry and parable, these stories (translated from Urdu) provide the unique perspectives on social, political and psychological issues that official histories ignore.

Equally at ease with polemic and lyricism, these writers mirror the events of their convoluted history – nationalism and independence, wars with India, the creation of Bangladesh, the death of Bhutto – in innovative and courageous forms. Influenced both by the Indian and Islamic traditions of their milieu and by the shocking impact of modernity, they are distinguished above all by their artistic integrity and intellectual honesty.

175 pages, 135 x 205 mm, ISBN 0 86356 039 3, paper